WOMEN WHO WON

BY THE SAME AUTHOR

The Gender Agenda

Women
Who Won

70 extraordinary women
who reshaped politics

Ros Ball

With illustrations by Emmy Lupin

unbound

First published in 2023

Unbound
c/o TC Group, 6th Floor King's House, 9–10 Haymarket, London SW1Y 4BP
www.unbound.com

© Ros Ball, 2023
Illustrations © Emmy Lupin

Text design by Patty Rennie

A CIP record for this book is available from the British Library

ISBN 978-1-80018-252-3 (hardback)
ISBN 978-1-80018-253-0 (ebook)

Printed in Italy by L.E.G.O. SpA.

1 3 5 7 9 8 6 4 2

MIX
Paper | Supporting
responsible forestry
FSC® C023419

Thank you to the Jo Cox Foundation,
a supporter of this book

THE **JO COX**
FOUNDATION

Jo Cox was a passionate campaigner, activist and humanitarian; a proud Yorkshire lass and internationalist; and a devoted mum, daughter, sister, wife, friend and MP.

The Jo Cox Foundation makes meaningful change on issues that Jo was passionate about. Like Jo, we believe that a kinder, fairer and more connected world is possible.

Find out more about our work at www.jocoxfoundation.org

Thank you to Clifford Chance,
a sponsor of this book

C L I F F O R D
C H A N C E

Clifford Chance is a global team of bright minds in a world-leading law firm, with a depth and range of expertise across five continents. As a single, fully integrated, global firm, the firm prides itself on having an approachable, collegial way of working, and its ground-breaking work. With over 30 offices across the world, they're uniquely placed to advise market-leading clients on complex, headlining deals. Its work has a real and meaningful impact.

Find out more at www.cliffordchance.com

Thank you to Action4Equality,
a sponsor of this book

Action 4 Equality
Scotland Ltd

Action4Equality campaigns for equal pay for public sector workers in Scotland. We have helped recover more than £1.5bn for low-paid women in Scotland over the last 20 years. Our Director Stefan Cross KC (Hon) has fought for equal pay for over 30 years and been instrumental in recovering over £4bn for more than 500,000 women in the UK. We welcome the opportunity to celebrate the achievements of these remarkable women.

Find out more at a4es.co.uk

Here's to democratically elected women.
May we know them. May we be them.
May we raise them.

Contents

Introduction.. 1

Sirimavo Bandaranaike 5

Jacinda Ardern 9

Ellen Johnson Sirleaf..13

Şafak Pavey..17

Alexandria Ocasio-Cortez....................................21

Shidzue Katō 25

Angela Merkel...29

Vijaya Lakshmi Pandit 33

Agathe Uwilingiyimana 37

Mary Robinson 41

Vigdís Finnbogadóttir..45

Sviatlana Tsikhanouskaya 49

Rose Lomathinda Chibambo................................55

Massouda Jalal 59

Corazon Aquino 63

Michelle Bachelet 67

Rawya Ateya 71

Julia Gillard 75

Peri-Khan Sofieva...79

Yulia Tymoshenko 83

Nicola Sturgeon 87

Ruth Mompati 91

Carol Martin 95

Clara Campoamor 99

Kamala Harris 103

Benazir Bhutto.. 107

Georgina Beyer 111

Violeta Barrios de Chamorro 115

Farrokhroo Parsa.. 119

Elvia Carrillo Puerto 123

Tsai Ing-wen... 127

Mia Amor Mottley 131

Constance Markievicz 135

Ethel Blondin-Andrew.. 139

Anna Boschek.. 143

Bidhya Devi Bhandari 147
Diane Abbott 151
Beatriz Merino 155
Hanan Ashrawi 159
Jóhanna Sigurðardóttir 163
Fiamē Naomi Mataʻafa 167
Shirley Chisholm 171
Margaret Thatcher 175
Megawati Sukarnoputri 179
Sahle-Work Zewde 183
Tina Anselmi 187
Vaira Vīķe-Freiberga 191
Sylvie Kinigi 195
Miina Sillanpää 199
Joyce Banda 203
Berta Pīpiņa 207
Portia Simpson-Miller 211
Graça Machel 215
Leyla Zana 219
Maureen Colquhoun 223
Cristina Fernández de Kirchner 227
Ella Koblo Gulama 231
Birtukan Mideksa 235
Jadranka Kosor 239
Isabel Ursula Teshea 243
Golda Meir 247
Jeannette Rankin 251
Gro Harlem Brundtland 255
Maria de Lourdes Pintasilgo 259
Laura Chinchilla 263
Iriaka Rātana 267
Marie Juchacz 271
Jahanara Shahnawaz 275
Eugenia Charles 279
Dilma Rousseff 283

Acknowledgements 287
A Note on the Author and Illustrator 289
Supporters 290

Introduction

Women Who Won is about women of the past but also women of the present and future. It profiles seventy women who have been political pioneers – the first in their nation to get elected, become a minister, take the highest office, or smash some other previously solid political glass ceiling. While I've been writing this book, history has been happening around me, and I've been able to add women who have been newly elected, such as Kamala Harris as the first woman to be vice president in the USA. It will be my pleasure if this book goes out of date as quickly as possible, but it will never be quick enough. How is it that countries like Japan, Italy, Mexico, South Africa and the USA have never had a woman lead them? The figures remain stark: 70 per cent of nations have only ever been led by a man.

Writing *Women Who Won* during the terrible Covid-19 pandemic has brought some extra insight into the picture for women world leaders since Sirimavo Bandaranaike was the world's first democratically elected woman prime minister in 1960, in what was then Ceylon. Sirimavo was mocked in the press and assumed to be incompetent, but in the twenty-first century we've seen headlines such as 'Women Leaders Have Shone During the Pandemic'. Studies have suggested that female political leaders have coped with the pandemic differently from and often better than men. My own take on this is that their sex is not necessarily the key factor here. The success may come from the fact that governments that are more diverse and listen to a multitude of voices are more successful – so a system which has enabled a woman to rise to the top is likely to have a winning approach. This only works if diversity is seen throughout the system, not just in one woman at the top of the tree. Having women in powerful positions is not inherently a good or a feminist thing if they don't use their power to support those without it, and there have certainly been plenty of those along the way. Like all politicians, women are not without flaws (and usually are allowed less leeway for them).

This is not an exhaustive list of every woman who broke a boundary as an elected politician, but you will find a lot of them are here – some you may like and some you may not. As well as those familiar to you, there are plenty that I think we haven't heard enough about or who I think we can learn from. I've particularly chosen to include women who left a positive legacy of stabilising democracy or opportunity for a future generation of women. In case you were wondering, the order of the profiles doesn't have any particular significance other than to create a journey around the world that flows well and keeps historical figures and present-day politicians jostling shoulder to shoulder.

While writing Women Who Won, I've reflected on what the women in these pages have in common. There is a historical pattern which is sometimes known as the 'widow's succession', where a woman takes the place of a man to whom she is related by marriage or birth. This is not to diminish the huge challenge of being a female political woman and managing to get elected, but is pointed out here to reflect how the voting public has been comfortable with (what appears to be) a more incremental change of husband/father to wife/daughter, and this has been replicated in parliaments across the world. It also speaks to the violence and grief that women in politics have frequently had to endure – assassinations are a regular feature in these stories. Next, I noticed that many of these women, but by no means all, grew up in households where they were treated equally with their brothers or encouraged to resist the usual gender roles. A not insignificant number also lost their father at a young age and they, or their mother, had to take on the role of working to earn for the family, suggesting the removal of the male 'head' of a household is noteworthy. Many also came from privileged backgrounds, which made their success easier, and this needs to shift if we want true representation. Finally, in a world where no country has yet achieved gender equality, my conclusion is that education is key. I've lost count of the number of women in this book who had their political awakening at university. It is a pivotal moment in life where horizons are expanded and the mind can range away from the confines of the home and its limited resources.

While these women may have a few things in common, they also have incredibly varied characteristics. So if you are looking for a woman who reflects your own personality, you'll find some who are quiet and cautious and others who are bombastic and confident, while still others are intellectual and precise. Every kind of personality can find a niche in politics and in making change – there is not one single formula for success.

With that in mind, I hope more than anything that this book is a way for women and girls who are interested in politics to imagine themselves in the shoes of these ancestors, and ultimately to see themselves as taking up those roles in the future. I hope very much that some of you reading this book will one day become women who won.

Sirimavo Bandaranaike

SRI LANKA

*Sirimavo Bandaranaike was the first woman in the world to
become a democratically elected head of government when she
became prime minister of Sri Lanka (then Ceylon) in 1960*

'History is full of examples of the disastrous consequences that
came upon such nations that changed their constitutions by giving
one man too much power.' These were the wise words of Sirimavo
Bandaranaike, who came to know the meaning of power more
than any woman before in the modern era. Born Sirima Ratwatte
in 1916, the suffix 'vo' is traditionally added to her name to denote
respect, which is fitting for the ultimate pioneer of women's political leadership.

Sirimavo was the eldest child of an influential family in what
was then the British-ruled colony of Ceylon. She attended a convent boarding school in the capital Colombo from the age of eight,
but her family were staunchly Buddhist. In 1940 she married
Solomon West Ridgeway Dias Bandaranaike, who was then minister of health. Sirimavo was her husband's confidante, and, on
her advice, he went on to establish the Sri Lanka Freedom Party
and was elected prime minister in 1956. His programme of government was to replace English with Sinhalese as the national
language and to make Buddhism the national religion. The pro-
posals were opposed by the Tamil-speaking Hindu minority, which
would consequently lead to years of bitter conflict. The family's
house was always open to visitors, and one day, in September 1959,
Sirimavo was in the garden when she heard a loud noise. Rushing

indoors, she saw a Buddhist monk had shot and fatally wounded her husband.

Her husband's death resulted in a vacuum of leadership, and Freedom Party seniors looked to Sirimavo to fill the gap. After initially refusing, she relented, leaving her little opportunity to grieve. As she pledged herself to continue her late husband's policies in public speeches, she frequently started to cry. The press cruelly dubbed her 'The Weeping Widow', and she faced attacks like the one by a member of the opposition who said, if she were to win the election, the prime minister's seat in parliament would have to be purified once a month, implying the stigmatisation of menstruation. Nevertheless, she secured victory in the election in 1960, becoming the world's first woman prime minister. *Time* magazine's coverage was typical of the sexist press she received: 'The real danger lay in the fact that she had not the foggiest idea of how to run a government. She kept the man-sized ministries of defence and foreign affairs for herself.' This dismissal of her was misguided: she would go on to transform herself into a career politician.

She carried out her party's programme of socialist policies, nationalising economic enterprises and making Sinhalese the official language. Against a background of economic crisis, she was defeated in the 1965 election, but she returned in 1970, implementing a new constitution that created an executive presidency and made Ceylon a republic renamed Sri Lanka. In 1980 parliament accused her of misusing her power while prime minister, and banned her from public office for seven years, during which the country descended into civil war. She later returned to parliament and saw her daughter Chandrika win the presidential election in 1994. Under her daughter's presidency, she served her third term as prime minister until her retirement. Her death from a heart attack on election day in 2000 seemed sadly apposite for a woman whose political career spanned four decades.

'CEYLON: Tearful Ruler', TIME, 1 August 1960, content.time.com/time/
    subscriber/article/0,33009,869666,00.html

'From the archive, 22 July 1960: Sri Lanka elects world's first woman prime minister', *Guardian*, 23 July 2013, www.theguardian.com/ theguardian/2013/jul/22/bandaranaike-first-woman-prime-minister

Jeyaraj, D.B.S., 'How Sirimavo Bandaranaike became the world's first woman prime minister 60 years ago', DBSJEYARAJ, dbsjeyaraj.com/ dbsj/archives/69557

Rambukwella, Harshana and Ruwanpura, Dr Kanchana N., 'The paradox of Sri Lanka's elite political women', Dangerous Women Project, 11 July 2016, dangerouswomenproject.org/2016/07/11/sri-lanka-political-women

Rettie, John, 'Obituary: Sirima Bandaranaike', *Guardian*, 11 October 2000, www.theguardian.com/news/2000/oct/11/guardianobituaries

'Sirimavo Bandaranaike', Britannica, www.britannica.com/biography/ Sirimavo-Bandaranaike

'Sirimavo Ratwatte Dias Bandaranaike', Sirimavo Bandaranaike, sirimavobandaranaike.org/madam-sirimavos-biography

Jacinda Ardern

NEW ZEALAND

*Jacinda Ardern was the youngest woman to be head of government when
elected prime minister of New Zealand in 2017 at age thirty-seven,
and the world's first elected leader to go on maternity leave*

Jacinda Ardern's rise to power was amazingly swift. Three months
before she was sworn in, she wasn't even leader of her party. Born
in 1980, she grew up in rural Waikato, a region of the upper North
Island of New Zealand, and has described herself as an 'acceptable nerd' in high school. It was her aunt, a longstanding Labour
Party member, who invited her to come campaigning. She quickly
became a volunteer coordinator and a champion door knocker, and
she became a party member aged eighteen. Raised as a Mormon,
she left the church in 2005 over its stance on LGBT+ rights.

After graduating from the University of Waikato in communication studies, majoring in politics and public relations, Jacinda
worked in roles across the Labour Party, including as an advisor
to Helen Clark, New Zealand's prime minister. She spent some
time in New York working in a soup kitchen and then in the
British civil service. In 2008 she was briefly president of the International Union of Socialist Youth, a role that took her around the
world.

Returning to New Zealand, Jacinda entered parliament on
Labour's list at the 2008 election (a list MP is selected by the party
rather than from a geographical constituency). At age twenty-eight
she was the youngest member of the House of Representatives and
became spokesperson for youth affairs.

Jacinda began 2017 as a list MP in an opposition party that was polling poorly, but in February that year she won a landslide by-election in the seat of Mt Albert and in March she was unanimously elected Labour's deputy leader. Then, less than eight weeks before general election day, Labour leader Andrew Little stepped down due to the party's poor polling, but didn't resign until he had Jacinda's word that she would stand. She was elected unopposed and campaigned on free university education, reductions in immigration and new programmes to alleviate child poverty.

The press called her popularity 'Jacindamania' and compared her to Barack Obama. She turned the party's chances around but not enough to win, and no party won a majority. Tense negotiations followed as parties tried to form a government. The 'queen-makers' were the New Zealand First party and the Green Party, who agreed to form a coalition, and Jacinda became the fortieth prime minister of New Zealand.

In 2018 Ardern became only the second elected leader in the world (after Pakistan's Benazir Bhutto) to give birth while in office. She set new standards by taking six weeks' maternity leave and shared the information that her partner would be a stay-at-home dad.

She earned international praise for her response to the 2019 terrorist attacks in Christchurch that killed fifty people in two mosques. Her government's handling of the Covid-19 pandemic, avoiding the mass deaths that devastated other countries, was thought to be a major factor in her party's comprehensive election victory in 2020. In 2023 she unexpectedly announced she was standing down, sparking global discussions about workplace burnout. She said, 'I'm leaving, because with such a privileged role comes responsibility – the responsibility to know when you are the right person to lead and also when you are not.'

When asked what qualities have underpinned her leadership, Jacinda singled out being 'really driven by empathy... when you think about all the big challenges that we face in the world, that's probably the quality we need the most'.

'Ardern, Jacinda', New Zealand Parliament, www.parliament.nz/en/pb/
hansard-debates/rhr/document/49HansS_20081216_00001012/
ardern-jacinda-maiden-statements

Blackwell, Geoff, 'Jacinda Ardern: "Political leaders can be both
empathetic and strong"', *Guardian*, 30 May 2020, www.theguardian.
com/world/2020/may/31/jacinda-ardern-political-leaders-can-be-
both-empathetic-and-strong

Dudding, Adam, 'Jacinda Ardern: I didn't want to work for Tony Blair',
Stuff, 27 August 2017, www.stuff.co.nz/national/politics/96123508/
jacinda-ardern-i-didnt-want-to-work-for-tony-blair

Gessen, Masha, 'Jacinda Ardern has rewritten the script for how a nation
grieves after a terrorist attack', *New Yorker*, 22 March 2019, www.
newyorker.com/news/our-columnists/jacinda-ardern-has-rewritten-
the-script-for-how-a-nation-grieves-after-a-terrorist-attack

Gillard, Julia and Okonjo-Iweala, Ngozi, *Women and Leadership: Real Lives,
Real Lessons*, Australia: Vintage Books, 2020

'Jacinda Ardern: Biography', New Zealand History, nzhistory.govt.nz/
people/jacinda-ardern

McLaughlin, Kelly and Hadden, Joey, 'New Zealand Prime Minister
Jacinda Ardern has been praised for her response to the coronavirus
pandemic', *Insider*, 15 April 2020, www.businessinsider.com/new-
zealand-prime-minister-jacinda-ardern-biography-2019-3?r=US&IR
=T#new-zealand-prime-minister-jacinda-ardern-has-been-praised-
for-her-response-to-the-coronavirus-pandemic-1

'Rt Hon Jacinda Ardern', Beehive, www.beehive.govt.nz/minister/
biography/jacinda-ardern

Ellen Johnson Sirleaf

LIBERIA

*Ellen Johnson Sirleaf was the first woman democratically
elected to serve as a head of state in Africa, and in 2005
was the first woman to be elected president of Liberia*

A few days after she was born, a family visitor saw Ellen and uttered
the words, 'This child will be great,' which Ellen refers to as a proph-
ecy. She said initially there was no reason to think the statement
would be accurate and her move towards leadership was slow and
included hardship. She was born in 1938 in Monrovia, the capital of
Liberia in West Africa, to parents who came from a background of
rural poverty but had worked hard to raise their prospects.

At seventeen Ellen married James Sirleaf, a young agronomist,
and they had four sons in rapid succession. As well as caring for
her family, Ellen worked as a bookkeeper, but when her husband
was offered the chance to pursue graduate studies in the USA,
Ellen went with him and studied accounting. When she returned to
Liberia she pursued a career in the ministry of finance. Ellen split
from her husband in 1961, citing his abuse in her autobiography.
She recounts an incident when her husband was angry that she
hadn't made his dinner and struck her with the butt of his gun. She
said her decision to leave was coloured by the realisation that her
classmates from school were leaving her behind as they achieved
in their careers. She said, 'One thing I had always believed in was
my own potential.'

Returning to the USA to study, Ellen earned an economics degree
and then a master's in public administration at Harvard. On her

return to Liberia she was appointed as assistant minister and later minister of finance in President William Tolbert's government. Her tenure was ended in 1980 by a coup d'état led by Samuel Doe, who became the military dictator of Liberia. He ordered the execution of President Tolbert and most members of his cabinet. Ellen was one of only four who survived. After resisting the new government, she fled to the USA, where she served in senior positions with the World Bank and later Citibank. She also worked as one of seven investigators of the Rwandan genocide.

Ellen returned to Liberia to campaign for the presidency in both 1985 and 1997, but was imprisoned and again went into exile in the USA, where she remained throughout the brutal Liberian civil war between the Doe government and a rebel group headed by warlord Charles Taylor. After Taylor went into exile in 2003 Ellen returned home to oversee preparations for democratic elections. She then ran for president and in 2005 became the first woman democratically elected to serve as a head of state in Africa.

Liberia had become one of the world's poorest nations, with huge levels of unemployment. As president, Ellen sought debt amelioration and the lifting of trade sanctions from the international community, and by late 2010 Liberia's debt had been erased. She established a right to free, universal primary education and secured funding for a new national university. She retired in 2017 after two terms in office and witnessed the country's first democratic transition of power in seventy-three years. In 2011 she won the Nobel Peace Prize for her non-violent struggle for the safety of women and for women's rights to full participation in peace-building work.

'Ellen Johnson Sirleaf', Academy of Achievement, achievement.org/ achiever/ellen-johnson-sirleaf

'Ellen Johnson Sirleaf', Britannica, www.britannica.com/biography/ Ellen-Johnson-Sirleaf

'Ellen Johnson Sirleaf: Biographical', The Nobel Prize, www.nobelprize. org/prizes/peace/2011/johnson_sirleaf/biographical

'Ellen Johnson Sirleaf: Interview', The Nobel Prize, www.nobelprize.org/prizes/peace/2011/johnson_sirleaf/interview

Gillard, Julia and Okonjo-Iweala, Ngozi, *Women and Leadership: Real Lives, Real Lessons*, Australia: Vintage Books, 2020

'Interviews: Ellen Johnson Sirleaf', The Freedom Collection, www.freedomcollection.org/interviews/ellen_johnson_sirleaf

Martin, Michael, 'Liberia president knew hardship before power', NPR, 8 April 2009, www.npr.org/transcripts/102866461

Skard, Torild, *Women of Power: Half a Century of Female Presidents and Prime Ministers Worldwide*, Bristol: Policy Press, 2014

Şafak Pavey

*In 2011 Şafak Pavey was the first disabled
woman elected to the Turkish National Assembly*

Şafak Pavey, who was born in the Turkish capital Ankara in 1976,
describes growing up in a family that always gave 'a great deal of
thought to how the majority of people face and resist difficul-
ties'. Şafak's mother was a journalist known for her investigative
reporting about corruption and government violence. Şafak moved
to Switzerland to study when she was nineteen and there she
experienced the defining moment of her life. She was at Zürich
train station helping a friend, who was travelling to a chemother-
apy session, to board the train. The train started moving with its
doors open so she pushed him into the carriage, but fell backwards
between the train and the platform. She lost her left arm and leg,
a particularly serious amputation with both limbs missing on the
same side, affecting stability. She said, 'Sometimes I am asked why
I am famous, and my answer always feels strange to me: "Because
I had an accident"... But I am now much stronger than those who
never fell in their lives.'

Şafak endured numerous operations and treatments, which
she describes as 'a lengthy hospital odyssey'. She and her mother
co-wrote a book about her experience called *Platform Number 13*,
which became a bestseller in Turkey. Şafak tried to resume her
studies in Istanbul but found the city too inaccessible. She said,
'As other disabled individuals frequently experience, the place society deemed suitable for me, and the place I thought I belonged

clashed constantly.' She left Turkey and enrolled at the University of Westminster in London while also working as a freelance journalist.

Şafak moved on to work for the United Nations, frequently working in conflict zones as a humanitarian aid worker. She has told stories of having to charge her electric prosthetic leg using a homemade wind-powered generator with parts collected by local Afghani children from old Soviet radios. She said she has proved that being disabled is not an obstacle to fieldwork, but she faced discrimination nonetheless, pushing her to develop employment policies for disabled staff at the UN.

In 2011 she was asked to stand for the Turkish parliament by the Republican People's Party and won in Istanbul province. She said it was the right time to stand because freedom of expression, women's rights and minority rights were in decline. In 2012 Şafak worked on a parliamentary inquiry about the gender separation of university dorms, leading to newspapers calling her an 'immoral woman'. A leading member of a political party's youth branch sent her a tweet saying: 'Allah took one of your legs and you haven't woken from the sleep of blasphemy.' Şafak wrote an open letter to the prime minister, urging him to remove the man from his post and he did. She said, 'This is the kind of hate speech stemming from the "deep culture" that millions of disabled people in my country face on a daily basis.'

Şafak stood down from parliament in 2017 due to ill health. Reflecting on what motivated her, she said, 'Many female politicians get intimidated by the aggressive behaviour of men. I don't. Not because I am a courageous person or anything, but because I see international standards and I see that they are worth fighting for.'

'Biyografi', Şafak, www.safakpavey.com/hakkimda/safak-hakkinda

Letsch, Constanze, 'Şafak Pavey: Turkey's "immoral woman" and the fight to wear trousers', Guardian, 9 February 2014, www.theguardian.com/politics/2014/feb/09/safak-pavey-turkeys-immoral-woman-trousers

Pavey, Şafak, 'Guest editorial: A redefined life: Şafak Pavey speaks at the 2013 ABJS meeting in Istanbul, Turkey', National Library of Medicine, 24 October 2013, www.ncbi.nlm.nih.gov/pmc/articles/PMC4160479

'Şafak Pavey', Indeks, www.indekskonusmaciajansi.com/en/safak-pavey

'Şafak Pavey – creating history, building a rights culture', I Know Politics, 1 April 2015, www.iknowpolitics.org/en/learn/knowledge-resources/interviews/şafak-pavey-creating-history-building-rights-culture

White, Jenny, 'Citizen Pavey', 3 Quarks Daily, 20 June 2011, 3quarksdaily.com/3quarksdaily/2011/06/citizen-pavey.html

Alexandria Ocasio-Cortez

UNITED STATES OF AMERICA

Alexandria Ocasio-Cortez was the youngest woman ever to serve in the United States Congress on her election in 2019 at the age of twenty-nine

Alexandria Ocasio-Cortez, or AOC as she's frequently known, has become one of the best-known women in American politics in the age of social media. Her popularity is global and her connection with a generation of young activists is key to that success. She started life in the Bronx, New York City, in 1989, born to a Puerto Rican family who moved to the suburbs looking for better schooling when she was five. She recalled being struck by the contrast between life in her new neighbourhood and her former home. Doing well at school, she described herself as a nerd with a strong interest in science.

Going to Boston University to study biochemistry, she changed her major to economics and international relations after her father died unexpectedly from cancer, leaving no will. Her mother took an extra job driving buses and Alexandria worked long hours as a waitress and bartender to support her family through the costs of settling her father's estate. She said watching her mother move out of New York City because of the cost of legal fees when their family home was at risk was the key thing that motivated her to go into politics. She interned for Democrat Senator Ted Kennedy's office and moved closer to grassroots politics through community organising for Latin youth in the Bronx.

She worked as an organiser for Bernie Sanders' presidential campaign in 2016, and in the same year took part in protests at

Standing Rock against the construction of the Dakota Access oil pipeline. She said, 'I saw how corporations had literally militarised themselves to do physical harm to American citizens, in particular Native peoples... we had to have a turning point.'

Alexandria was asked to run by an organisation putting forward candidates who wouldn't accept political donations from corporate campaign committees, and in 2018 she was the first party candidate to challenge veteran Democrat Joe Crowley's seat in fourteen years. The campaign was a huge challenge, with the disparity between their fundraising pots standing at ten to one. Alexandria organised a grassroots campaign, including a powerful video that began with her saying, 'Women like me aren't supposed to run for office,' which went viral. She rejected corporate donations, relying on small donors, and caused a huge upset when she won against Crowley. She went on to dispatch the Republican Anthony Pappas at the election and was sworn in in January 2019.

On entering the House of Representatives, Alexandria began her tenure by introducing legislation for a 'Green New Deal', a policy package to cut carbon while creating jobs and boosting the economy. She has continued to advocate for social, racial, economic and environmental justice, maintaining an activist position. She was one of the first to call for President Donald Trump's impeachment after his supporters staged a violent assault on the Capitol building in January 2021, following the 2020 election.

She coasted to victory for a second term in office, creating speculation about her future political ambitions, but she doesn't necessarily see higher office as the key to her aims. She explained, 'I wake up, and I'm like, what would be the most effective thing to do to advance the power and build the power of working people?'

'Alexandria Ocasio-Cortez', Iowa State University Archives of Women's Political Communication, awpc.cattcenter.iastate.edu/directory/alexandria-ocasio-cortez

'Alexandria Ocasio-Cortez', Ocasio-Cortez, ocasio-cortez.house.gov/about

Kurtzleben, Danielle, 'Rep. Alexandria Ocasio-Cortez releases Green New Deal outline', *All Things Considered*, NPR, 7 February 2019, www.npr.org/2019/02/07/691997301/rep-alexandria-ocasio-cortez-releases-green-new-deal-outline?t=1647606570129

Newman, Andy, Wang, Vivian and Ferré-Sadurní, Luis, 'Alexandria Ocasio-Cortez emerges as a political star', *New York Times*, 27 June 2018, www.nytimes.com/2018/06/27/nyregion/alexandria-ocasio-cortez-bio-profile.html

Ruiz, Michelle, 'AOC's next four years', *Vanity Fair*, 28 October 2020, www.vanityfair.com/news/2020/10/becoming-aoc-cover-story-2020

Scahill, Jeremy, 'An interview with Alexandria Ocasio-Cortez', The Intercept, 27 June 2018, theintercept.com/2018/06/27/an-interview-with-alexandria-ocasio-cortez-the-young-democratic-socialist-who-just-shocked-the-establishment

Wang, Vivian, 'Alexandria Ocasio-Cortez: a 28-year-old Democratic giant slayer', *New York Times*, 27 June 2018, www.nytimes.com/2018/06/27/nyregion/alexandria-ocasio-cortez.html

Shidzue Katō

JAPAN

*In 1946 Shidzue Katō was among the first
women elected to the Diet of Japan*

A pioneer of the birth control movement, Shidzue Katō said her calling was to give women control over reproduction, allowing them to plan their families rather than suffer the consequences of unwanted children. She herself was fortunate to be born into an affluent, ex-samurai family in Tokyo in 1897. Her father was a mining engineer, and her mother, who had been educated at a missionary school, brought international ideas into their home.

In 1914 she graduated from the exclusive Joshi Gakushūin (Peeresses' School), and when she was seventeen, Count Ishimoto Keikichi asked to marry her. She was apparently far from delighted, but the pair met, and she consented to the match. Her husband was a Christian humanist interested in social reforms and together they moved to the coal mines in Kyushu where he was a mining engineer. Shidzue was confronted with a way of living she had never experienced. Her home was a tumbledown hut and mine workers lived alongside her in appalling conditions. Men crawled naked along hot, narrow passages, while women, pregnant or with small children, 'wriggled like worms' while dragging baskets of coal. The women had to cope with successive pregnancies, with babies dying in large numbers. She and her husband worked to improve the lives of the labourers who worked twelve hours a day, particularly women who then went home to care for their big families.

After three years both Shidzue and her husband suffered breakdowns in their health, and travelled to the United States. Encouraged by her husband, Shidzue enrolled in secretarial school, a highly unusual move for a Japanese woman with her background. Meeting Margaret Sanger at the beginning of the 1920s proved a turning point. Sanger was an American activist who dedicated her life to legalising birth control and making it universally available. Shidzue returned to Japan the next year and began campaigning for safe family planning and other women's rights. In 1932 she founded the fully staffed Birth Control Consultation Centre, which was stocked with contraceptives for the women of Tokyo.

The military regime in Japan was fiercely hostile to ideas of limiting the country's growing population. In December 1937 Shidzue was arrested for promotion of 'dangerous thoughts', and she spent two weeks in prison. The records of her clinic were confiscated and it was shut down, temporarily halting the birth control movement in Japan until after the Second World War.

Her husband changed his stance over time and expected his wife to return to a traditional role while he increasingly supported the goals of Imperial Japan. She divorced him, and supported herself and her two sons through writing, later marrying socialist leader Katō Kanju. In 1946, after Japanese women were given the right to vote, she and her husband were both elected to the House of Representatives for the Japan Socialist Party. She was then elected to the House of Councillors in 1950.

Alongside supporting women's reproductive health, Shidzue worked for abolition of the feudal family code, which supported a system dominated by men, and persuaded the prime minister to revoke Japanese claims on Korea. She served for twenty-eight years and continued to be active in public life until the age of 100, when she published a second autobiography. She died aged 104 in 2001.

Blacker, Carmen, 'Obituary: Shizue Kato', *Guardian*, 1 February 2002, www.theguardian.com/news/2002/feb/01/guardianobituaries. socialsciences

Hopper, Helen M., *A New Woman of Japan: A Political Biography of Kato Shidzue*, Oxfordshire: Taylor & Francis, 2019

'Japanese feminist leader Kato dies', *Midland Daily News*, 21 December 2001, www.ourmidland.com/news/article/Japanese-Feminist-Leader-Kato-Dies-7210936.php

'Katō Shidzue', University of Pittsburgh, www.japanpitt.pitt.edu/glossary/katō-shidzue

'Kato, Shidzue 1897–2001', Encyclopedia.com, www.encyclopedia.com/arts/educational-magazines/kato-shidzue-1897-2001

'Shidzue Ishimoto Kato (1897–2001)', Museum of Contraception and Abortion, muvs.org/en/topics/pioneers/shidzue-ishimoto-kato-1897-2001-en

Angela Merkel

GERMANY

*In 2005 Angela Merkel was the first woman
to be elected as chancellor of Germany*

As chancellor, Angela Merkel said that one of her most difficult decisions was to find the right time to stop. This is typical of her famously cautious leadership style, sometimes attributed to her growing up in East Germany, where citizens living under communism had to exercise caution in daily life. Weeks after her birth in West Germany in 1954, her family moved to East Germany because her father, a Lutheran theology student, had been offered a pastorate. East Germany, or the German Democratic Republic, had been founded in 1949 when the country was split in two with the Allied forces in control of the West and the Soviets of the East. In the East the population were spied on by the Stasi, the secret police, in order to repress opposition.

Angela enjoyed films and books sent or smuggled from the West and wore Levi's jeans that couldn't be bought in the East. Always interested in politics, she listened to West German radio in secret and dreamed of visiting the British Houses of Parliament in London. She decided to pursue physics at university because, as she put it, 'there, the truth isn't so easily bent'. She studied in Leipzig and married fellow student Ulrich Merkel but divorced four years later. When applying for a job at an engineering college, she was famously met by a Stasi officer wanting to recruit her, but she declined, saying she couldn't keep secrets.

In 1989 the Berlin Wall came down and Angela was involved in the democracy movement as people scrambled to start political parties. She became an East German government spokesperson, impressing colleagues with her calm ability to handle journalists. Next came the reunification of Germany in 1990. Angela's party joined the West German centre-right Christian Democrats (CDU) and she was elected to the Bundestag (parliament). CDU Chancellor Helmut Kohl saw her potential and mentored her as she rose rapidly.

When Kohl was caught in a scandal, she called for his resignation, and in 2000 was chosen to lead the CDU herself. Her rise to be leader of a male-dominated, largely Catholic party, as a Protestant woman, was a surprise to many. Though some disregarded her, she had an inner confidence, saying, 'I've never underestimated myself. There's nothing wrong with being ambitious.' In the elections in 2005 there was no clear winner, but Angela beat Gerhard Schröder to become chancellor of a 'grand coalition' government.

Just a few years after taking office, the financial crisis of 2008 hit global markets and was followed by the European debt crisis, when several Eurozone member states were unable to repay government debt. Angela's management of the crisis led to her reputation as the key power player in Europe, but her critics disagreed with her largely austerity-based approach. In 2011, when the civil war escalated in Syria, triggering a flood of refugees to Europe, Angela refused to close German borders. She said, 'If Europe fails on the question of refugees, then it won't be the Europe we wished for.'

Angela served four terms as chancellor, and in 2019 announced that term would be her last. She remains a popular figure in Germany due to her pragmatic leadership, which kept her at the head of Europe's most powerful economy for sixteen years.

'Angela Merkel', New World Encyclopedia, www.newworldencyclopedia. org/entry/Angela_Merkel

'Angela Merkel: Germany's shrewd political survivor', BBC, 3 June 2019, www.bbc.co.uk/news/world-europe-23709337

Cain, Aine, 'Angela Merkel will serve 4 more years as the chancellor of Germany', *Insider*, 24 September 2017, www.businessinsider.com/angela-merkel-early-career-2017-9?r=US&IR=T

'Chancellorship of Angela Merkel', Britannica, www.britannica.com/biography/Angela-Merkel/Chancellorship

Kurbjuwelt, Dirk, 'A wall separates Merkel and the land of her dreams', *Spiegel International*, 12 April 2010, www.spiegel.de/international/germany/a-difficult-friendship-with-obama-a-wall-separates-merkel-and-the-land-of-her-dreams-a-688393.html

Marr, Andrew, 'The making of Angela Merkel, a German enigma', BBC, 24 September 2013, www.bbc.co.uk/news/magazine-24159595

Mayer, Catherine, 'Merkel's moment', TIME, 11 January 2010, content.time.com/time/magazine/article/0,9171,1950954-2,00.html

Pazzanese, Christina, 'Angela Merkel, the scientist who became a world leader', *The Harvard Gazette*, 28 May 2019, news.harvard.edu/gazette/story/2019/05/those-who-have-known-angela-merkel-describe-her-rise-to-prominence

Skard, Torild, *Women of Power: Half a Century of Female Presidents and Prime Ministers Worldwide*, Bristol: Policy Press, 2014

Whalan, Roscoe, 'Angela Merkel: How a poor girl from East Germany rose to become the "Empress of Europe"', ABC News, 24 September 2021, www.abc.net.au/news/2021-09-24/empress-of-europe-angela-merkel-legacy-in-germany/100465618

Yasar, Abdulaziz Ahmet, 'From Helmut Kohl's "little girl" to the most powerful woman in the world', TRTWorld, 20 October 2018, www.trtworld.com/europe/merkel-helmut-kohl-s-little-girl-to-the-most-powerful-woman-in-the-world-21234

Vijaya Lakshmi Pandit

INDIA

In 1937 Vijaya Lakshmi Pandit was the first woman
to hold a cabinet position in pre-independent India

Once a friend chastised Vijaya Lakshmi Pandit's father about the way he was raising his daughter, asking, 'Why is she being educated according to foreign standards and being given so much freedom? Do you intend to make her into a lawyer like yourself?' Her father asked her directly if she would like to read law, leaving her clear in the knowledge that the option was open to her. This was the atmosphere this bright young woman was born into, in 1900 in Allahabad, in her politically active family home. Her father was a lawyer and politician who would become president of the Indian National Congress, the political party of the independence movement, during the independence struggle, and her mother would be an advocate of civil disobedience against the British Raj, encouraging women to make salt in breach of British salt laws (production and distribution of salt was monopolised by the British and included a heavy tax). Her older brother, Pandit Jawaharlal Nehru, would be the first prime minister of India. Their large household included extended family such as her niece Indira Gandhi, who would also go on to become prime minister.

Educated alongside her brothers, Vijaya Lakshmi was tutored by an English governess, though as the nationalist movement gained momentum the family boycotted British education. When she was nineteen, a young barrister named Ranjit Sitaram Pandit proposed, but 'I didn't know what to say,' she recalled, 'I'd only known him for three days.' However, she accepted, and their close family friend Mahatma Gandhi was the first person to bless the couple after they were married.

Vijaya Lakshmi and her family increasingly devoted their time to the Indian National Congress. Her activities included organising and leading processions and delivering fiery speeches, which led to her arrest and a year in prison when her third child was three.

In 1937, she won election to the provincial legislature of the United Provinces and was made the minister of local self-government and public health. She was struck by the inadequacy of the health department and became dedicated to improving health-care for women, instituting programmes for clean drinking water, milk for children, and playgrounds throughout India.

In 1939, alongside colleagues in Congress, she resigned to protest against the involuntary participation of British India in the Second World War. She was imprisoned again in 1942 along with her husband and colleagues for issuing a resolution demanding the British 'Quit India'. Her husband's health deteriorated in prison and he died shortly after being released. Indian law allowed nothing for her as a widow, with all inheritance going to male relatives. In the first Indian elections her brother, Prime Minister Nehru, made inheritance for women one of the major items.

Post-independence, Vijaya Lakshmi had a pre-eminent diplomatic career. She was Indian ambassador to the Soviet Union, Washington and Mexico, and the first woman president of the United Nations General Assembly in 1953. She came out of political retirement to oppose her niece, Prime Minister Indira Gandhi, when the latter called a state of emergency and suspended democracy from 1975 to 1977. In the elections that followed, her niece was ousted and reportedly never forgave her aunt.

Upon Vijaya Lakshmi's death in 1990 at the age of ninety, Indian President Ramaswami Venkataraman described her as a 'luminous strand in the tapestry of India's freedom struggle'.

Jha, Avishek, 'Vijaya Lakshmi Pandit, Nehru's younger sister who slammed Indira for Emergency', The Print, 18 August 2018, theprint.in/theprint-essential/vijaya-lakshmi-pandit-a-freedom-fighter-diplomat-and-politician/100649

Mehrotra, Rajiv, 'In conversation – Vijaya Lakshmi Pandit', YouTube, 10 April 2015, www.youtube.com/watch?v=LmFZoGSPi6o&t=166s

'Pandit, Vijaya Lakshmi (1900–1990)', Encyclopedia.com, www.encyclopedia.com/women/encyclopedias-almanacs-transcripts-and-maps/pandit-vijaya-lakshmi-1900-1990

'Remembering Nehru's sister Vijaya Lakshmi Pandit', India Today, 7 June 2021, www.indiatoday.in/education-today/gk-current-affairs/story/remembering-nehru-s-sister-vijaya-lakshmi-pandit-who-was-imprisoned-thrice-during-the-indian-freedom-struggle-1317554-2018-08-18

Scroll.in, 'Women in Constituent Assembly | Episode 2: Vijaya Lakshmi Pandit', YouTube, 29 January 2018, https://youtu.be/2SjFHY2UsqU

'Vijaya Lakshmi Pandit', Constitution of India, www.constitutionofindia.net/constituent_assembly_members/vijaya_lakshmi_pandit

'Vijaya Lakshmi Pandit (India)', United Nations, www.un.org/en/ga/president/bios/bio08.shtml

Agathe Uwilingiyimana

RWANDA

*In 1993 Agathe Uwilingiyimana was the first
woman to serve as prime minister of Rwanda*

The Rwanda of Agathe Uwilingiyimana's childhood was a place
of ongoing tension. Belgian colonial rule had left a legacy of ethnic division between the majority Hutus and the minority Tutsis.
Agathe was born in 1953 in Nyaruhengeri, a village in Butare province. She walked for two hours every day to get to primary school,
where she showed great promise. Thanks to her brother, who
worked to support her, she went on to a Catholic girls' secondary
school in the capital Kigali and she was among the first women to
obtain a bachelor's degree from the University of Rwanda, majoring in chemistry. She married a school classmate in 1976 and had
the first of five children the following year.

Agathe taught high-school maths and science and made a name
for herself by setting up a credit cooperative society for the school
staff. The government was seeking influential local leaders from the
turbulent south of Rwanda, and in 1989 she was appointed to a post
as director for small- and medium-sized industries in the ministry of commerce. In 1990, the Rwandan Patriotic Front (RPF), who
were mostly Tutsi refugees, invaded Rwanda from Uganda and the
country was plunged into civil war. In January 1992 Agathe joined
the moderate Republican and Democratic Movement (MDR) and
four months later was appointed minister of education. Her belief
in equal educational opportunity, regardless of ethnic group, disrupted the status quo and made her an enemy of some, but popular

with others. Her MDR colleague Jean Marie Vianney Uwihanganye said, 'She was a very eloquent public speaker and had a unique way of getting her point across, which endeared her to the masses.'

The MDR organised elections for the leadership of the strategic Butare province, where Agathe beat Jean Kambanda by 300 to 50 votes. Agathe's supporters have suggested that Kambanda's disdain towards her took root from this defeat. In the coming years Kambanda, who became prime minister in 1994, would plead guilty to genocide. It was a highly dangerous time to be a woman in government and Agathe was attacked in her home on multiple occasions, including in April 1993, when assailants broke into her home and beat and raped her.

After a tentative peace agreement in July 1993, a meeting between the president and the opposition parties working under a power-sharing agreement was held. Agathe was agreed as the prime minister, but political infighting caused her dismissal from the post after less than a month, although she remained as caretaker while there was no clear way forward. In April 1994 the president's plane crashed under suspicious circumstances, and Hutu soldiers used this as a reason to attack Tutsis and Hutu moderates. Agathe called for calm but Hutu soldiers had already surrounded her home.

She was killed and sexually assaulted on 7 April 1994, along with her husband, an aide and the ten Belgian United Nations peacekeepers guarding her. Her death paved the way for Hutu extremists to take over the government and carry out a genocide targeting Tutsis, members of opposition political parties, human rights activists and journalists. An estimated 500,000 to a million Rwandans were slaughtered in about 100 days. Agathe's children escaped with the help of a UN peacekeeper and grew up in Switzerland in foster care.

Agathe is remembered as a pioneering politician and someone who tried to reconcile ethnic differences when others chose violence.

Burnet, Jennie, 'Uwilingiyimana, Agathe', Oxford Research Encyclopedias, 26 March 2019, oxfordre.com/africanhistory/view/10.1093/acrefore/9780190277734.001.0001/acrefore-9780190277734-e-487

Butare, Innocent, *Une jeune femme sur un bateau ivre: Agathe Uwilingiyimana du Rwanda*, Cameroon: Langaa RPCIG, 2019

Damon, Lisa, 'Une jeune femme sur un bateau ivre', review, African Books Collective, www.readafricanbooks.com/reviews/une-jeune-femme-sur-un-bateau-ivre

de la Croix Tabaro, Jean, '23 years later, meet ex-PM Agathe Uwilingiyimana's children', KTPress, 31 January 2017, www.ktpress.rw/2017/01/23-years-later-meet-ex-pm-agathe-uwilingiyimanas-children

— 'Agathe Uwiringiyimana: A heroine unfortunate to have lived in evil era', *The New Times*, 5 May 2014, www.newtimes.co.rw/section/read/75086

Johnson, Elizabeth Ofosuah, 'The only top Rwandan female public officer was a prime minister and she was assassinated in 1994', F2F Africa, 26 July 2018, face2faceafrica.com/article/the-only-top-rwandan-female-public-officer-was-a-prime-minister-and-she-was-assassinated-in-1994

Skard, Torild, *Women of Power: Half a Century of Female Presidents and Prime Ministers Worldwide*, Bristol: Policy Press, 2014

Mary Robinson

IRELAND

*In 1990 Mary Robinson was the first
woman to be elected president of Ireland*

The only girl in a family of five, Mary Robinson cites her grandfather's profession as a lawyer as influential on her interest in justice, as well as the fact she was 'wedged between four brothers'. Born in 1944, she didn't receive equal treatment with her brothers and recalls, after she was caught climbing a tree, that her grandfather shouted, 'You have to be sent away to school, you are not becoming a young lady.' Mary consequently went to a Catholic girls' boarding school, after which she briefly considered becoming a nun. Deciding the convent wasn't for her, she studied law at Trinity College Dublin. She graduated with first-class honours, which led to a master's at Harvard during the Vietnam War, the experience of which, she said, shook every assumption she had grown up with.

She was appointed auditor of the Law Society in Dublin in 1967 and in her combative inaugural address she argued to legalise divorce, contraception and homosexuality and to increase women's and children's rights. She was admitted to the Bar in 1967 and became the youngest professor of law at Trinity College, aged just twenty-five. Her marriage to a Protestant man of whom her parents didn't approve led to them boycotting her wedding, though she was reconciled with them in the following months.

Under the system in the Irish Seanad (the upper house of parliament), universities hold six seats. It was in the Dublin University constituency that Mary was elected as a member of the Irish Labour

41

Party in 1969 and held the seat for twenty years. However, she resigned the Labour Party whip due to a disagreement over the 1985 Anglo-Irish Agreement and became an independent. She had tried twice, without success, to get elected to a parliamentary seat when, in 1990, she was surprised to be asked by the Labour Party to stand as president. She said she would think about it over the weekend and used the time to look at the Irish constitution. She said although the role is not political, she was convinced that because the president is elected by the people, she would be able to advocate for 'all the things that matter' and 'be close to people'.

Mary was elected Irish president in 1990 and served for seven years. She said, 'So many women cried on the day of my inauguration, at the very fact that a woman could be president.' The election was a turning point for Ireland, summed up by the story Mary's driver told her when he asked his wife to make him a cup of tea and she told him, 'Make your own tea, things have changed around here.'

Mary focused on reconciliation, humanitarian issues and women's rights during her time in office. She was the first Irish head of state to make official visits to Britain, as well as regularly visiting Northern Ireland. She used her position to fight to make contraception legally available despite the enemies it made her. The local Catholic bishop denounced her from the pulpit in her hometown while her parents were sitting in the congregation.

In 1997 Mary stepped down as president to become United Nations High Commissioner for Human Rights. She went on to focus her work on climate justice through her foundation and is Adjunct Professor for Climate Justice at Trinity College Dublin.

_____

Burke, Helen and O'Leary, Olivia, *Mary Robinson: The Authorised Biography*, London: Hodder & Stoughton, 1998

Gillard, Julia, 'Mary Robinson on being the first female President of Ireland', *A Podcast of One's Own*, 5 May 2021, play.acast.com/s/ a-podcast-of-ones-own/maryrobinsononbeingthefirstfemale presidentofireland

The Late Late Show, ' "Things have changed around here – make your own tea!" Mary Robinson', YouTube, 20 November 2020, www.youtube.com/watch?v=UypUo6tbQ1I

Liswood, Laura A., *Women World Leaders: Fifteen Great Politicians Tell Their Stories*, London: Pandora, 1995

'Mary Robinson', American University of Beirut, www.aub.edu.lb/doctorates/recipients/Pages/MaryRobinson.aspx

'Mary Robinson', Britannica, www.britannica.com/biography/Mary-Robinson

'Mary Robinson – global world leader', The Mary Robinson Centre, www.maryrobinsoncentre.ie/biography.html

RTÉ, 'Mary Robinson talks about why she ran for the presidency', YouTube, 15 September 2012, www.youtube.com/watch?v=FQm1V7YJYRE

RTÉ, 'Saturday night with Miriam: Mary Robinson interview', YouTube, 25 July 2011, www.youtube.com/watch?v=URJf7pBXDi4

Skard, Torild, *Women of Power: Half a Century of Female Presidents and Prime Ministers Worldwide*, Bristol: Policy Press, 2014

Vigdís Finnbogadóttir

ICELAND

*Vigdís Finnbogadóttir was the first woman in the
world to be a democratically elected president when
she was elected the president of Iceland in 1980*

'I hear it all the time, it changed everything... Women thought, if she can, I can,' said Vigdís Finnbogadóttir, reflecting on her place in history. Though she says she never expected to win, her background gave her a grounding to succeed. Born in 1930 in Reykjavík, she came from a family of professionals: her mother was a nurse and chaired Iceland's national nurses' association, while her father was a port engineer and later a university professor.

After graduating from Reykjavík grammar school in 1949 having majored in languages, Vigdís went to France and Denmark to study and returned to the University of Iceland, where she later taught French and theatre history. She married in 1954 but divorced seven years later.

She was a founder of the first experimental theatre group in Iceland while also working as a tour guide and establishing 'cultural tourism', promoting Iceland to foreign journalists and filmmakers. From 1971 to 1972 she presented French lessons and theatrical performances on television, which gave her a popular national profile. At this time she adopted a daughter, the first single woman in Iceland allowed to do so, setting the tone for her role as a woman breaking with traditions of the past. From 1972 Vigdís was director of the Reykjavík Theatre Company and she continued to assert her influence on civic society on the Advisory Committee on Cultural Affairs in Nordic Countries and was elected its chair in 1978.

The president of Iceland is a non-governmental role and is elected by popular vote for four-year terms. When the presidential election arrived in 1980, it was in the context of a growing women's movement for equality. In 1975 the women of Iceland had mounted a strike, refusing to work, cook and look after children for a day. In Reykjavík 90 per cent of women joined the march, leaving banks, factories and some shops closed, as well as schools and nurseries. Many fathers took their children to work as they had no other option. Vigdís said of the historic day, 'It completely paralysed the country and opened the eyes of many men.'

The first call for Vigdís to run for election was in a letter to the editor of an Icelandic newspaper. A Reykjavík housewife explained that a group of women had come to the conclusion that she should stand. Vigdís initially said no but was swayed by support from all over the country. There was strong nationwide interest in the election campaign, with voter turnout registered at 90.5 per cent. Vigdís won with 33.6 per cent of the national vote, narrowly beating her three male opponents. When a large crowd gathered outside her home to congratulate her, Vigdís emerged wearing a hand-knitted dress that she had been presented with by a supporter during the election campaign and that she had promised to wear if she won.

Her popularity grew, and she held the position for four consecutive terms until her retirement in 1996, serving for sixteen years in all. In her role as president, Vigdís advocated for the environment, national culture and equality for women and girls. After her presidency, she became the founding chair of the Council of Women World Leaders.

'Finnbogadóttir, Vigdís (1930–)', Encyclopedia.com, www.encyclopedia. com/women/encyclopedias-almanacs-transcripts-and-maps/ finnbogadottir-vigdis-1930

Liswood, Laura A., *Women World Leaders: Fifteen Great Politicians Tell Their Stories*, London: Pandora, 1995

Skard, Torild, *Women of Power: Half a Century of Female Presidents and Prime Ministers Worldwide*, Bristol: Policy Press, 2014

'Vigdís Finnbogadóttir', Britannica, www.britannica.com/biography/Vigdis-Finnbogadottir

'Vigdís Finnbogadóttir, b. 1930', nordics info, nordics.info/show/artikel/vigdis-finnbogadottir-b-1930

Sviatlana Tsikhanouskaya

BELARUS

*In 2020 Sviatlana Tsikhanouskaya was the first
woman to be 'the national, chosen president' of Belarus*

Sviatlana Tsikhanouskaya is a startlingly new recruit to politics. When her husband was jailed while trying to run for president in 2020, she took his place. At the time of writing, authoritarian leader Alexander Lukashenko has been in power since 1994 and is described as the last dictator in Europe. Sviatlana said a wall of fear holding Belarus back has disappeared and that 'everything has changed, we are bound to win'.

Sviatlana was born in 1982 when Belarus was part of the Soviet Union, and grew up in a granite-mining town in the south of the country. She said, 'Like every family, we talked about politics... But in the kitchen, whispering, so no one could hear.' She went to college to train as an English teacher and met Sergei Tikhanovsky in the nightclub he owned, and they married. Their first child was profoundly deaf, and she gave up work to care for him, moving the family to the capital, Minsk, so he could have cochlear implants. She spent eight years teaching him so he could catch up with his peers, and planned to return to her career.

When the Covid-19 pandemic arrived, President Lukashenko mocked his citizens for being afraid and failed to put protective policies in place. Sviatlana's husband was a popular vlogger, touring the country interviewing people frustrated with the regime. As his popularity grew, he announced he would stand as a presidential candidate. When he was suddenly jailed, causing him to miss the deadline to stand, Sviatlana put herself forward as a form of protest. Initially she remained quiet, but when election officials refused to register two other key candidates, she was pushed to step forward. Sviatlana headed a team of three women – herself, Maria Kalesnikava, the campaign manager of a jailed candidate, and Veranika Tsapkala, the wife of a candidate who had been forced into exile. They became well known for a power pose, making a heart symbol, a power fist and a peace sign.

President Lukashenko claimed he wasn't initially threatened by Sviatlana's challenge, saying, 'Our constitution was not written for a woman, and our society isn't ready to vote for a woman.' Despite her lack of experience, Sviatlana was a powerful speaker, drawing tens of thousands of supporters to rallies. Her election promise was to free political prisoners and to step down after six months to hold a new, free presidential vote. As her popularity grew, the danger to her increased; she got a phone call threatening to put her children in an orphanage and send her to jail. She said she was scared to continue, but decided that 'There must be a symbol of freedom.'

On election day her allies were certain she had won, but Lukashenko announced he had more than 80 per cent of the vote. Protesters took to the streets and were beaten and tear-gassed by riot police. The next day Sviatlana filed a protest at the result and Lukashenko's head of security detained her, giving her a choice to go to prison or leave the country. She was exiled to Lithuania while tens of thousands of people were detained, with reports of prisoners being beaten, electrocuted and raped.

Sviatlana has toured numerous countries gathering support for a free Belarus. She said her role should be described as 'the national, chosen president' and her aim is to build a new country.

Bennetts, Marc, 'Svetlana Tikhanovskaya: housewife steps into election fight with Belarus strongman Lukashenko', The Times, 6 June 2020, www.thetimes.co.uk/article/svetlana-tsikhanouski-housewife-gears-up-for-election-fight-with-belarus-strongman-rgtnr7qmv

Butler, Katherine, 'Svetlana Tikhanovskaya: from "Chernobyl child"

in Ireland to political limelight', *Guardian*, 11 August 2020,
www.theguardian.com/world/2020/aug/11/svetlana-tikhanovskaya-
from-chernobyl-child-in-ireland-to-political-limelight

Filkins, Dexter, 'The accidental revolutionary leading Belarus's uprising',
New Yorker, 6 December 2021, www.newyorker.com/magazine/
2021/12/13/the-accidental-revolutionary-leading-belaruss-uprising

Gessen, Masha, 'Sviatlana Tsikhanouskaya is overcoming her fears',
New Yorker, 13 December 2020, www.newyorker.com/news/the-new-
yorker-interview/sviatlana-tsikhanouskaya-is-overcoming-her-
fears

Karmanau, Yuras, 'Ex-teacher hopes to free Belarus from president's iron
fist', AP, 4 August 2020, apnews.com/article/virus-outbreak-
alexander-lukashenko-belarus-international-news-elections-
c9ba5be40472ac02673a4d8bdec8a9ea

Lynott, Laura, 'Belarus opposition leader Svetlana Tikhanovskaya
meets her Irish "Chernobyl children" host family and raises Ryanair
hijacking', *Irish Independent*, 13 July 2021, www.independent.ie/irish-
news/politics/belarus-opposition-leadersvetlana-tikhanovskaya-
meets-her-irish-chernobyl-children-host-family-and-raises-ryanair-
hijacking-40649187.html

Mackinnon, Amy, 'Belarus's unlikely new leader', FP, 6 August 2021,
foreignpolicy.com/2021/08/06/belarus-tsikhanouskaya-lukashenko-
new-leader-europe

Mackinnon, Mark, 'As a "Chernobyl child," Belarus's opposition leader
learned to speak for the vulnerable – and forged a friendship with
a Nova Scotia professor', *Globe and Mail*, 10 September 2020,
www.theglobeandmail.com/world/article-as-a-chernobyl-child-
belaruss-opposition-leader-learned-to-speak

Miller, Christopher, 'She challenged Europe's last dictator in Belarus
and was forced into exile', BuzzFeed News, 8 September 2020,
www.buzzfeednews.com/article/christopherm51/belarus-svetlana-
tikhanovskaya-interview-lukashenko-protests

Roth, Andrew, 'Sviatlana Tsikhanouskaya: "Belarusians weren't ready for
this level of cruelty"', *Guardian*, 9 August 2021, www.theguardian.com/
world/2021/aug/09/sviatlana-tsikhanouskaya-belarusians-not-ready-
cruelty-lukashenko-belarus

Sommerlad, Joe, 'Who is Europe's "last dictator" Alexander Lukashenko?', *Independent*, 28 February 2022, www.independent.co.uk/news/world/europe/alexander-lukashenko-belarus-ukraine-russia-b2024868.html

Walt, Vivienne, 'How a Belarusian teacher and stay-at-home mom came to lead a national revolt', *TIME*, 25 February 2021, time.com/5941818/svetlana-tikhanovskaya-belarus-opposition-leader

Rose Lomathinda Chibambo

MALAWI

In 1964 Rose Lomathinda Chibambo was the first
woman to become a cabinet minister in Malawi

When Lomathinda Ziba was growing up in what was then Nyasaland, the national mood was shifting towards independence from colonial occupation. The East African country was a British protectorate controlled by a white governor appointed by the British government and responsible to the Colonial Office. Rose was born in 1928; the name Lomathinda means 'snatched from the grave', and she would always be someone who defied the odds.

Her husband, Edwin Chibambo, described her as 'my rose', leading her to adopt the name as her own. They married in 1947 and, while pregnant with her first child, Rose finished her primary education at night school. She noticed her husband coming home late from work and discovered he was attending meetings to discuss the need for the country's independence to avoid being pushed into a Federation of Rhodesia and Nyasaland, which would continue to impose a British governor-general. When she asked him if women attended these meetings, he said he had never seen a woman there but she was very welcome, in his opinion. Rose said she told herself, 'Instead of going to join the men alone, I will talk to my fellow women. Then I went around mobilising women.' She organised protests on issues affecting women, but the Federation was imposed on the country in 1953.

Rose's husband, who was a civil servant, was transferred to the capital Blantyre that year, which Rose thought was to stop her 'rabble-rousing'. However, it was there that she joined the local branch of the Nyasaland African Congress (NAC), became the treasurer and went on to form the women's wing. Tensions rose as the NAC leader, Hastings Kamuzu Banda, toured the country pushing for independence. Reacting to the unrest it caused, the governor-general declared a state of emergency, ordered the arrest of the majority of the NAC leaders and the banning of the party. Rose was not immediately arrested as she was heavily pregnant with her fifth child, but two days after she gave birth she was taken from the hospital to a maximum-security prison. She and her baby remained in prison for thirteen months, only being released when negotiations for independence started in 1961. Elections were finally held in 1964 and Rose became the only woman in parliament as well as minister for community and social development.

The euphoria of independence was short-lived. President Banda began making decisions at odds with his freedom-fighting colleagues, including an alliance with apartheid South Africa and recognising Portugal as 'owners' of Mozambique. Confronted by his ministers, Banda called a vote of confidence, which he won, but when she challenged him, Rose heard the news of her dismissal via the radio. Speaking to defend herself in parliament, she received no support and fled to Zambia with her husband. She stayed in exile for thirty years, separated from some of her children.

Rose returned only when Banda was defeated in new democratic elections. She worked in business and to support the large numbers of Malawians suffering in the HIV/AIDS epidemic. Rose felt she didn't receive recognition from her nation for the sacrifices she made for independence, but four years before her death in 2016, at the age of eighty-six, she was commemorated on the 200 kwacha banknote.

Lipenga, Timwa, *Lomathinda: Rose Chibambo Speaks*, Malawi: Logos – Open Culture, 2019

Madimbo, Maggie, *Transformative and Engaging Leadership: Lessons from Indigenous African Women*, New York: Palgrave Macmillan US, 2016

Phoya, Muti, 'In honour of Rose Lomathinda Chibambo', Africa Is a Country, 29 January 2016, africasacountry.com/2016/01/in-honor-of-rose-lomathinda-chibambo

Power, Joey, *Political Culture and Nationalism in Malawi: Building Kwacha*, Rochester: University of Rochester Press, 2010

'Rose Chibambo, 1928–2016', Scotland Malawi Partnership, www.scotland-malawipartnership.org/news/rose-chibambo-1928-2016

'Rose Chibambo dies aged 86: Malawi first female minister – she is on banknote', *Nyasa Times*, 12 January 2016, www.nyasatimes.com/rose-chibambo-dies-aged-86-malawi-first-female-minister-she-is-on-banknote

'Rose Chibambo (Malawi)', PeaceWomen Across the Globe, wikipeacewomen.org/wpworg/en/?page_id=3118

Massouda Jalal

AFGHANISTAN

*In 2002 Massouda Jalal was the first woman to
run for the office of the president of Afghanistan*

Dr Massouda Jalal, who was born in 1964, said she challenged the
status quo even as a child: 'I never had the feeling that as a girl or as
a woman, I [was] less competent, never! I had three brothers, but
I was usually better than them.' In a country that is known for its
conservative attitudes to women, after scoring the second-highest
marks in the national college entrance exam of Afghanistan, she
attended Kabul University and studied medicine.

Massouda began her career in a mental health clinic but that was
closed as the country descended into civil war following the end of
the Soviet occupation in 1989. She moved into paediatrics in Kabul
children's hospital and taught at the university medical school. The
rise to power of the newly formed Islamic militia, the Taliban, in
1996 brought with it the suppression of women's education and
employment. Women were required to be fully veiled and were not
allowed outside alone. Forced into her home, Massouda said, 'It
was just announced... We had no choice.' She practised medicine
from her home and began work for the United Nations World Food
Programme in the women's department. She set up bakeries for
widows who had no income and advocated for girls' education,
putting her in regular conflict with the Taliban, who arrested her.
With the intervention of the UN, she was released. Despite her vulnerable position, she stayed in Afghanistan. 'All the time I received
threats,' she said. 'It was very hard.'

After the fall of the Taliban in 2001, Massouda emerged as a leading voice for women in Afghan society and won a seat as representative of her Kabul neighbourhood to the 2002 emergency Loya Jirga ('grand council') of Afghanistan. In a huge contrast to the life women had been expected to live until very recently, she put herself forward as interim presidential candidate. It was the first time a woman had run. She said, 'After 5,000 years of history, I am the first.'

Massouda ran as an independent against the US-backed favourite Hamid Karzai, who had the support of armed factions. She said her platform was on behalf of the people who had suffered from many years of war: 'They need somebody to give them kindness, to give them love, to give them sympathy, to give them trust, confidence, and to treat their wounds, to give them easier life, to be helpful to people, to be honest to people.' She finished second, winning the support of 171 delegates to Karzai's 1,295.

She worked to include human rights and rights for women in the 2003 drafting of the constitution of Afghanistan. She ran for president again in 2004 and her campaign was captured in the documentary *Frontrunner*. Coming in sixth, she took a role as minister of women's affairs in Karzai's government.

After government Massouda founded the Jalal Foundation to protect women's rights. She ran for the presidential office again in 2019, resulting in attacks on her and her family members. As the Taliban once again took over Afghanistan in 2021, she was forced to flee her country, taking exile in the Netherlands.

BeautyandtheEastTV, 'The Afghan woman who ran for president – Dr. Massouda Jalal', YouTube, 17 April 2009, www.youtube.com/watch?v=0OmwaMXHVgA

'Biography of Dr. Masooda Jalal', Afghanistan Online, www.afghan-web.com/biographies/biography-of-dr-masooda-jalal

Bos, Truus, 'Afghan woman takes on presidential politics', NBC News, 7 September 2004, www.nbcnews.com/id/wbna5931226

Clark, Kate, 'Profile: Massouda Jalal', BBC, 12 June 2002, news.bbc.co.uk/1/hi/world/south_asia/2040523.stm

'Dr. Massouda Jalal', Massouda Jalal, www.massoudajalal.com/about

'Jalal, Masooda Mrs. Dr. Massoda Masoda', Afghan Biographies, www.afghan-bios.info/index.php?option=com_afghanbios&id= 743&task=view&total=2524&start=973&itemid=2

'Massouda Jalal', Prabook, prabook.com/web/massouda.jalal/2279842

Pincock, Stephen, 'Massouda Jalal, presidential candidate in Afghanistan', *The Lancet*, Vol. 364, 2004, 1307, www.thelancet.com/ pdfs/journals/lancet/PIIS0140-6736(04)17174-2.pdf

Shankar, Kunal, 'Interview | I hope the Taliban will learn from their past mistakes: Massouda Jalal', The Wire, 7 September 2021, thewire.in/ south-asia/massouda-jalal-interview

Weaver, Caroline, 'Profile of Afghanistan's Minister of Women's Affairs, Massouda Jalal', VOA News, 28 October 2009, www.voanews.com/a/ a-13-2005-03-10-voa8-66917787/377147.html

Corazon Aquino

THE PHILIPPINES

In 1986 Corazon Aquino was the first woman
to be elected president of the Philippines

Maria Corazon Cojuangco described herself as a reserved child, born in 1933 into a politically prominent family from Tarlac province. Her mother was a pharmacist, her father was a congressman and both her grandfathers had been senators. Cory, as she was known, remembers handing out cigars to political leaders who visited her father. She was valedictorian of her private school class before going to high school in the United States. There she joined the junior Republicans and volunteered during the 1948 presidential election. Returning to the Philippines to attend law school, she met fellow student Benigno 'Ninoy' Aquino Jr and left to marry and raise their family.

Ninoy was elected as a governor and then to the Senate, becoming increasingly successful at opposing dictator President Ferdinand Marcos. Ninoy was expected to win the next election, but when Marcos declared martial law in 1972, Ninoy was arrested and sentenced to death. He wrote in his diary that he was ashamed that he broke down while Cory never dropped a single tear. She later said it was because she was 'fortified with tranquillisers'.

With Ninoy in prison, Cory campaigned and delivered speeches on his behalf, a significant transition for someone who had previously remained in the background. After years of imprisonment Ninoy was released into medical exile and the family lived in the USA for three years. After he recovered, he returned to the

Philippines but was assassinated by soldiers after stepping off the plane. Cory said, 'I followed a few days later, no longer as a house-wife but as a widow... It was the greatest funeral since Gandhi.' An estimated 2 million people lined the streets.

Cory participated in peaceful demonstrations named the 'People Power Revolution'. It became clear she could mobilise the electorate and she received a million signatures in support of her candidacy for president. Marcos called an election in 1986 with Cory as his opponent, making it clear it was a dangerous path for her to take. Cory said Marcos was 'A coward for threatening to take me out with a single bullet; and a loser, because I promised him no more than a single ballot in return.'

When election polls closed, Cory was believed to be the winner, but the government declared for Marcos. Hundreds of thousands of citizens protested in her campaign colour of yellow, and two of Marcos's key military leaders revolted. After weeks of polit-ical unrest both Cory and Marcos were inaugurated as president by their supporters, but by the end of the day Marcos had fled the country.

Cory saw her mandate as restoring democracy and created a new constitution limiting presidential powers, ratified by a landslide popular vote. Marcos's supporters tried to remove her from office many times, with seven military revolts resulting in more than 150 deaths. Critics argued that Cory failed to undertake fundamental economic or social reforms, and her popularity declined as she faced outcries over economic injustice and political corruption.

Cory served only one term, and, when President Fidel Ramos took over, Cory said it was 'one of the proudest moments of my life... This was what my husband had died for... This moment is democracy's glory: the peaceful transfer of power without blood-shed, in strict accordance with law.'

'9 things you may not know about Corazon Aquino,' FillipiKnow,
    29 April 2022, filipiknow.net/facts-about-cory-aquino

Alexander, Kerri Lee, 'Corazon Aquino', National Women's History Museum, www.womenshistory.org/education-resources/biographies/corazon-aquino

Aquino, Corazon, 'Speech upon receipt of the Fulbright Prize – Oct. 11, 1996', Iowa State University Archives of Women's Political Communication, 11 October 1996, web.archive.org/web/20210528113740/awpc.cattcenter.iastate.edu/2017/03/21/speech-upon-receipt-of-the-fulbright-prize-oct-11-1996

'Corazon Aquino', Britannica, www.britannica.com/biography/Corazon-Aquino

Liswood, Laura A., *Women World Leaders: Fifteen Great Politicians Tell Their Stories*, London: Pandora, 1995

Skard, Torild, *Women of Power: Half a Century of Female Presidents and Prime Ministers Worldwide*, Bristol: Policy Press, 2014

Michelle Bachelet

CHILE

*In 2006 Michelle Bachelet was the first
woman to be elected president of Chile*

In her presidential victory speech, Michelle Bachelet reflected on
Chile's violent past while looking to the future, saying, 'Because
I was a victim of hate, I've dedicated my life to turning hate into
understanding, tolerance, and – why not say it? – love.' Her journey
to this point was painful and she was internationally recognised for
her conciliatory stance.

Verónica Michelle Bachelet Jeria was born in the capital,
Santiago, in 1951; her mother was an archaeologist and her father
a general in the Chilean Air Force. Her father's job meant the family
moved frequently and she grew up in the military world. In the early
1960s he was assigned to the Washington embassy for two years,
where Michelle was influenced by the US civil rights movement and
learned fluent English.

In 1973 her father was arrested for opposing the military coup
that ousted President Salvador Allende and brought General
Augusto Pinochet to power, with secret support from the CIA,
America's foreign intelligence service. Her father was tortured for
several months before he suffered a heart attack and died in prison.
Michelle, then a medical student at the University of Chile, said her
world fell apart overnight: 'When I walked down the street, people
who had been very close to us crossed to the other side so as not
to have to see us.'

Michelle was arrested, along with her mother, and sent to a

secret prison where she was tortured. She was blindfolded and tied to a chair for long periods and told that her mother would be executed. Thanks to lobbying by an influential relative, in 1975 they were allowed to leave Chile. They first lived in exile in Australia, and then in East Germany, where they were offered asylum. Michelle eventually returned to studying medicine, became active in socialist politics and got married.

Returning to Chile in 1979, it was still difficult for Michelle to get employment due to her family history, but she joined a medical clinic that treated victims of torture and political repression who couldn't get treatment elsewhere. After Pinochet was ousted from power in 1990, she moved into politics, first becoming minister of health and then as the first woman to lead the ministry of defence in Ricardo Lagos Escobar's government.

Her 2005 presidential campaign focused on greater equality and social inclusion. Her campaign had to deal with her status as an agnostic, divorced mother of three, which presented a challenge to the traditionalist Roman Catholic establishment. Nonetheless, she beat her nearest rival in a presidential run-off with 53 per cent of the vote. She was the first popularly elected South American woman president whose political career was established independently of a husband.

Her first term was marked by an ambitious agenda of better healthcare, pension reform and poverty reduction with a cabinet with equal numbers of women and men. Prevented by the constitution from serving a consecutive term, in 2010 Bachelet moved on to become head of the newly established UN Women.

She returned to win a second presidential term in 2013, and her achievements included tax reform, free university education for low-income students, creating a ministry of women and decriminalising abortion.

Gillard, Julia and Okonjo-Iweala, Ngozi, *Women and Leadership: Real Lives, Real Lessons*, Australia: Vintage Books, 2020

Leimbach, Dulcie, '"Don't try to be a superwoman": an interview with Michelle Bachelet', PassBlue, 31 May 2018, www.passblue.com/2018/05/31/dont-try-to-be-a-superwoman-an-interview-with-michelle-bachelet

'Michelle Bachelet', Britannica, www.britannica.com/biography/Michelle-Bachelet

'Michelle Bachelet', Columbia University World Leaders Forum, worldleaders.columbia.edu/directory/michelle-bachelet

'Michelle Bachelet', Encyclopedia.com, www.encyclopedia.com/journals/culture-magazines/bachelet-michelle

'Michelle Bachelet Biography', Encyclopedia of World Biography, www.notablebiographies.com/newsmakers2/2007-A-Co/Bachelet-Michelle.html

Rohter, Larry, 'A leader making peace with Chile's past', New York Times, 16 January 2006, www.nytimes.com/2006/01/16/world/americas/a-leader-making-peace-with-chiles-past.html

Skard, Torild, Women of Power: Half a Century of Female Presidents and Prime Ministers Worldwide, Bristol: Policy Press, 2014

Rawya Ateya

EGYPT

In 1957 Rawya Ateya was one of the first
two women elected to parliament in Egypt

Rawya Ateya was heavily involved in politics at a young age. She was born in 1926 and her father was the secretary general of the Wafd party, a nationalist party that was instrumental in gaining Egyptian independence from Britain in 1952. He was imprisoned as a result of his political activities and she remembered visiting him there as a child. At the age of ten Rawya led demonstrations of her school's students to protest against British colonial rule. On one occasion she was hit by a bullet and fainted; she recalled, 'I found myself in the hands of Mrs Huda Shaarawy. She carried me, and brought me into the headquarters of the General Women's Union, the pioneer of the women's movement... I was raised politically in their hands.'

She studied for a diploma in education and psychology, and went on to receive a master's degree in journalism and a second diploma in Islamic studies. Making the most of her education, she worked as a teacher for fifteen years and as a journalist for six years, all the while continuing volunteering activities.

President Gamal Abdel Nasser announced that women would be able to vote and be nominated to stand for parliament in the new 1956 constitution. That year, Rawya became the first woman to be commissioned as an officer in Egypt's Liberation Army and went on to help train thousands of women in first aid and nursing during the Suez Crisis, when Egypt was invaded by Israel, Britain and

France. She led a women's commando unit and later, during the Arab–Israeli War of 1973, established an association to care for the families of fighters, earning her the moniker 'mother of the martyred combatants'.

In 1957 opinion polls showed that a majority of Egyptian men were opposed to the idea of women standing for seats in parliament. Nonetheless, Rawya decided to put herself forward for election despite the sexism she faced at the time, saying, 'I was met with resentment for being a woman. Yet I talked to them and reminded them of the prophet's wives and families until they changed their opinions.'

Her strategy for the electoral campaign was to be as visible as possible: 'I began to go down to the voters, and I was riding in a jeep, and I was dressed in the commando uniform, and people greeted me with ululating, drums, and clans, and everyone was seeking to see me as the first woman to run in elections in this place, and thus I felt that I pulled the rug from under the feet of the male competitors.'

Rawya won and during her time in politics she pushed for the advancement of women's rights and towards equality for women in the labour force, most notably through a two-month maternity leave with full salary. In 1958 she presented a law abolishing polygamy, though it did not pass due to strong opposition by other members of parliament.

In the National Assembly elections in 1959, Rawya failed to renew her membership to parliament, but she joined the dissolved National Party and nominated herself again for membership in the People's Assembly in the 1984 elections. She was successful and became a member of the Egyptian parliament for the second time. She died in 1997 at the age of seventy-one.

Goldschmidt, Arthur Jr and Goldschmidt, Arthur, *Biographical Dictionary of Modern Egypt*, Boulder: Lynne Rienner, 2000

'Here's the story of Rawya Ateya: first woman parliamentarian in the Arab world', Egyptian Streets, 16 October 2020, egyptianstreets.com/

2020/10/16/heres-the-story-of-rawya-ateya-first-woman-parliamentarian-in-the-arab-world

'Rawya Ateya took her seat in the National Assembly', The Asian Age, 14 July 2017, dailyasianage.com/news/73502/rawya-ateya-took-her-seat-in-the-national-assembly

Sullivan, Earl L., *Women in Egyptian Public Life*, Syracuse: Syracuse University Press, 1986

Zevi, Tullia, 'Gals should get more than equal rights in Egypt', *Pittsburgh Press*, 30 January 1959, news.google.com/newspapers?id=_AofAAAAIBAJ&sjid=95UEAAAAIBAJ&pg=7241,4072960

Julia Gillard

*In 2010 Julia Gillard was the first woman
to be elected prime minister of Australia*

Like many women in this book, it took time for Julia Gillard to
see herself as a politician. She explained, 'It was a slow dawning
over time that it would be a fantastic way of putting my values into
action – and realising that someone like me could do it.' Born in
1961 in Wales in the UK, she suffered from bronchial pneumonia
which added to her family's decision to migrate to Australia for the
warmer climate. Settling in Adelaide, her family regularly discussed
politics, and her views were affected by her father's inability to take
up a school scholarship because he had had to work to support his
family. She said, 'It's always burned in me a sense of indignation...
That someone who had the capacity to go on to higher education... could still have that opportunity ripped from their hands by
economic circumstance.'

At university Julia was introduced to the Labor Party club by
a friend and she became president of the Australian Union of
Students, giving her a formative political experience. She earned de-
grees in law and arts and joined a private law practice specialising in
employment law. In 1996 Julia left her job to serve as chief-of-staff
to the opposition leader of the State of Victoria and quickly made
her own move to stand for election, going on to win a federal seat
in 1998. After four successive election defeats for the Labor Party,
2007 brought election success and Julia was sworn in as minister for
education and the country's first woman deputy prime minister.

In 2010 she challenged Prime Minister Kevin Rudd to a leadership contest from which he later withdrew, knowing he couldn't win. Gillard was sworn in as prime minister but said she wouldn't move into the official home of the PM until she was endorsed by the electorate, and so a general election was called. The election race was extremely tight, and after failing to win an outright majority, Julia gained the support of three independent MPs and one Green MP and formed a minority government.

As prime minister of the twelfth-biggest economy in the world, in the aftermath of the global financial crisis that began in 2008, Julia inherited a difficult brief. Her work in office included education reform, a carbon emissions trading scheme, healthcare reform, the first national scheme to care for people with disabilities, building the National Broadband Network and a commission into institutional responses to child sexual abuse. She received strong criticism for her stance on asylum seekers, immigration and reduction in job-seeker payments.

Julia famously delivered a parliamentary speech on misogyny in response to opposition leader Tony Abbott, which she says was spontaneous, handwritten on the spot and fuelled by anger at the treatment she received from rival politicians and the press. In her speech she said, 'The leader of the opposition says that people who hold sexist views and who are misogynists are not appropriate for high office. Well, I hope the leader of the opposition has got a piece of paper and he is writing out his resignation. Because if he wants to know what misogyny looks like in modern Australia, he doesn't need a motion in the House of Representatives, he needs a mirror.'

The speech went viral and made her name around the world. She subsequently said, 'There was a time where I was a little resentful that all those years in politics, and all of that work... apparently came down to one moment in time, one speech. But I'm reconciled with it now, and I understand that when people are writing things about me – including writing my obituary, hopefully in many years to come – that it's going to feature in there.'

After being defeated in a leadership ballot in 2013, Julia resigned as prime minister. Her work after politics has focused on gender equality, including becoming the chair of the Global Institute for Women's Leadership at King's College London as well as being the chair of Wellcome, a global charitable foundation which supports science to solve urgent health challenges.

Beard, Alison, 'Life's work: an interview with Julia Gillard', *Harvard Business Review*, November–December 2019, hbr.org/2019/11/lifes-work-an-interview-with-julia-gillard

Gillard, Julia and Okonjo-Iweala, Ngozi, *Women and Leadership: Real Lives, Real Lessons*, Australia: Vintage Books, 2020

Harmon, Steph and Siddeek, Amaani, '"It took on a life of its own": the story behind Julia Gillard's misogyny speech', *Guardian*, 7 February 2020, www.theguardian.com/tv-and-radio/2020/feb/07/it-took-on-a-life-of-its-own-the-story-behind-julia-gillards-misogyny-speech

'Julia Gillard', Britannica, www.britannica.com/biography/Julia-Gillard

'Julia Gillard: during office', National Archives of Australia, www.naa.gov.au/explore-collection/australias-prime-ministers/julia-gillard/during-office

'Julia Gillard Interview Transcript', Australian Story, 6 March 2006, web.archive.org/web/20100609093523/www.abc.net.au/austory/content/2006/s1585300.htm

'Julia Gillard's Official Biography', Julia Gillard, www.juliagillard.com.au/about-julia

Marriner, Cosima, 'Gillard reveals: it was the go-girl factor', *Sydney Morning Herald*, 26 November 2007, www.smh.com.au/national/gillard-reveals-it-was-the-go-girl-factor-20071126-gdrolr.html

Skard, Torild, *Women of Power: Half a Century of Female Presidents and Prime Ministers Worldwide*, Bristol: Policy Press, 2014

'Transcript of Julia Gillard's speech', *Sydney Morning Herald*, 10 October 2012, www.smh.com.au/politics/federal/transcript-of-julia-gillards-speech-20121010-27c36.html

Peri-Khan Sofieva

GEORGIA

*Peri-Khan Sofieva is thought to be the first democratically
elected Muslim woman in the world*

Most of what is known about Peri-Khan Sofieva are stories handed
down by her family and village elders. Her exact date of birth is
unknown, but it was some time during 1884 that she was born in
the village of Karajala in Georgia, then part of the Russian Empire,
the only girl in a family of nine. There is one key piece of evidence
of her life – her signature in the official records listing her as a
regional representative, and a Georgian press clipping noting the
'happy event' of the election of a Muslim woman in 1918.

Family members recall her with the name 'Peri-Khan the man'
and describe her as an imposing figure armed with a Mauser pistol
and smoking a hookah pipe, something considered controversial
for women. Taking a leadership role in her family from a young age,
she would rise to lead village affairs, mediate in disputes, and read
from the Quran at weddings and funerals. Her descendants say that
during the Tsarist era she persuaded the Imperial Russian government to run a new railway line close to the village, and when she
had negotiations and discussions with men 'she was the dominant
one'. She had become head of the village in all but name, but that
would come.

In May 1918, amid the collapse of Imperial Russia, members of
the Georgian National Council gathered in the capital Tbilisi's main
thoroughfare, and declared Georgia an independent republic. The
First Democratic Republic of Georgia would last for less than three

years, but was a trailblazer in social democracy. Elections were held with the participation of both men and women, a constitution was implemented, and anti-discrimination laws for ethnic and religious minorities were passed and women's rights were established.

One of the new republic's first acts was to hold local elections, creating democratic accountability at village level. Peri-Khan ran as an independent in the elections in 1918 and won, competing against candidates from Georgia's nationwide political parties. Her victory shows how much local influence she must have had, and she is described as 'unique' by the historian who discovered Peri-Khan's name in the archives.

In 1919 Georgia elected five women to parliament, becoming only the tenth country in the world to do so, but it was not to last. In early 1921 Soviet Russia's Red Army invaded Georgia and the republic was overthrown and replaced with a Bolshevik regime.

Peri-Khan's family say that despite the Bolshevik takeover, her authority over local affairs remained. Stalin's Great Terror came to the village in 1937 and five of Peri-Khan's brothers were taken from their homes and executed as 'enemies of the people'. Peri-Khan raised and cared for her brothers' orphaned children and dedicated herself to protecting them and ensuring they were able to progress in life, despite the discrimination that children of 'enemies of the people' experienced.

Peri-Khan died in 1953. Rakhshanda Sofieva, the widow of Peri-Khan's nephew, said, 'Nobody could suppress her, not the Soviet government, not anyone else.'

'Akakli Khvadagiani. Mother of calligraphy – Parikhanim Sofiyeva', Türk Dünyasi info, 25 September 2017, web.archive.org/web/20181201201722/http://www.turkinfo.org/2017/09/25/akakli-xvadagiani-qarayazi-anasi-p%C9%99rixanim-sofiyeva

Dunbar, William, 'The world's first democratically elected Muslim woman was from Georgia', eurasianet, 8 March 2018, eurasianet.org/the-worlds-first-democratically-elected-muslim-woman-was-from-georgia

Embassy of Georgia to US, '#GEORGIA100', Medium, 5 June 2018, medium.com/@GeorgianEmbassy/georgia100-622d8e640157

'The First Democratic Republic of Georgia', National Archives of Georgia, archive.gov.ge/en/sakartelos-pirveli-demokratiuli-respublika

Jones, Stephen, 'Remembering Georgia's First Republic', Civil.ge, 25 May 2018, civil.ge/archives/242414

Yulia Tymoshenko

UKRAINE

*In 2005 Yulia Tymoshenko was the first
woman to serve as prime minister of Ukraine*

If politics is partly about getting noticed, then Yulia Tymoshenko
was the master of it in the 2000s. Her distinctive braided hair and
her campaigning style saw her described as a 'political atom bomb'
when she appeared on the international stage. She was born in
1960, an only child whose father left when she was young; she grew
up watching her mother work multiple jobs to support their small
family. She majored in cybernetic engineering and economics at
university and married Oleksandr Tymoshenko while still a teenage
student. Together they started a chain of video rental stores, a sign
of changing times in the Soviet Union under Mikhail Gorbachev's
market reforms. When Ukraine became an independent country
after the collapse of the Soviet Union in 1991, Yulia moved into the
energy sector, holding key commercial leadership positions which
garnered her the nickname the 'Energy Queen'.

She switched to politics with relative ease and was elected to parliament in 1996. In 1999 she founded her own left-leaning party,
Batkivshchyna (Fatherland), and by the end of the decade she was
deputy prime minister to Viktor Yushchenko, and in charge of the
energy sector. In 2001 she spent several weeks in jail, accused of
forging customs documents and smuggling gas – charges of which
she was subsequently cleared. It was at this point that she changed
image, adopting her blonde trademark peasant-style braid, reportedly to emphasise national identity.

Yulia was a key player in the Orange Revolution in 2004. With her ally Viktor Yushchenko she led mass peaceful protests when Viktor Yanukovych, backed by Russian president Vladimir Putin, was announced as winner of the presidential election. The protesters argued the result was fraudulent and 500,000 people descended on Kyiv's Independence Square. After courts ruled the result invalid, Viktor Yushchenko won the presidency on a pro-Western, anti-Russian platform. Yulia was appointed as prime minister and said she would work to get Ukraine into the European Union without alienating Russia, challenge corruption and create an independent judiciary. However, her relationship with the president quickly deteriorated and he sacked her later that year.

Her party performed well in the 2007 election and she was reappointed as prime minister, campaigning for changes to the constitution, but she continued to battle with President Yushchenko. This distraction from the global economic crisis and the work of improving life for people in Ukraine became the largest criticism levelled against her during her tenure.

She lost to Viktor Yanukovych in the 2010 presidential elections and in 2011 was found guilty of abuse of authority. It was ruled she had signed overpriced gas contracts with Russia and she was sentenced to seven years in prison. The human rights organisation Amnesty International said the case was politically motivated, and she complained of violence against her while in prison and held a hunger strike.

A second popular uprising erupted when Yanukovych attempted to create closer ties with Russia rather than an agreement with the EU as approved by parliament. In the face of public violence Yanukovych fled to Russia and Yulia was freed.

Although she stepped straight back into politics, her support had not endured and she failed in her bid for the presidency in 2019. Critical of the winner, Volodymyr Zelenskyy, she swung behind him following the Russian invasion of Ukraine in 2022 and has remained in the country, working to support the war effort.

Bateson, Ian, 'The fall and troubled rise of a Ukrainian populist', *Atlantic*, 28 March 2019, www.theatlantic.com/international/archive/2019/03/ukraine-tymoshenko-president-populist/585868

Fletcher, Martin, 'The woman who went head to head with Putin – and survived', *The Times*, 30 April 2022, www.thetimes.co.uk/article/the-woman-who-went-head-to-head-with-putin-and-survived-9t98tzlgw

Harding, Luke, 'Yulia Tymoshenko: Ukraine's bruised firebrand', *Guardian*, 6 May 2012, www.theguardian.com/theobserver/2012/may/06/profile-yulia-tymoshenko-ukraine

Karimi, Faith, 'Yulia Tymoshenko walks out of prison, and back into Ukrainian politics', CNN, 23 February 2014, edition.cnn.com/2014/02/23/world/europe/ukraine-yulia-tymoshenko-profile/index.html

Kis, Oksana, '"Beauty will save the world!": Feminine strategies in Ukrainian politics and the case of Yulia Tymoshenko', www.yorku.ca/soi/_Vol_7_2/_HTML/Kis.html

'Profile: Yulia Tymoshenko', Al Jazeera, 23 May 2014, www.aljazeera.com/news/2014/5/23/profile-yulia-tymoshenko-2

'Profile: Yulia Tymoshenko', BBC, 23 May 2014, www.bbc.co.uk/news/world-europe-15249184

Skard, Torild, *Women of Power: Half a Century of Female Presidents and Prime Ministers Worldwide*, Bristol: Policy Press, 2014

Tymoshenko, Yuliya, 'The Iron Lady as liberator', Project Syndicate, 9 April 2013, www.project-syndicate.org/commentary/margaret-thatcher-and-soviet-freedom-by-yuliya-tymoshenko

'Yulia Tymoshenko', Britannica, www.britannica.com/biography/Yulia-Tymoshenko

Nicola Sturgeon

UNITED KINGDOM

In 2014 Nicola Sturgeon was the first woman
to be elected first minister of Scotland

Nicola Sturgeon described herself as an introverted child who hid under a table at her fifth birthday party. Born in 1970, she grew up in her parents' council house in the west of Scotland and as a working-class girl she was expected to join the Labour Party, particularly as the Scottish National Party (SNP) lacked popularity at the time, but this logic didn't follow for Nicola and she joined the SNP at the age of sixteen. She distributed leaflets during the 1987 election, when the SNP only returned three MPs to the Westminster parliament.

Nicola has repeatedly said that three-time British prime minister Margaret Thatcher's record in government was 'the motivation for my entire political career'. She says the Thatcher era's unemployment and closure of heavy industry 'gave me a strong sense of social justice; it was wrong for Scotland to be governed by a Tory government that we hadn't elected'. She campaigned for the SNP while studying law in Glasgow, the first member of her family to go to university. Law clearly was never a long-term career aim because she stood, unsuccessfully, in the 1992 UK general election aged just twenty-one. She ran and lost again in 1997 but the incoming Labour government had promised to devolve more powers across the UK. A referendum was held, which led to a parliament in Scotland being reinstated and in its first elections Nicola won a seat.

In the Scottish election in 2007 the SNP emerged as the largest party, and with their leader Alex Salmond still sitting in Westminster, Nicola led the party in Edinburgh. She served as cabinet secretary for health, where she abolished prescription charges. The dramatic change in the political landscape from Nicola's youth was clear to see when the SNP won an outright majority in the 2011 election. They had campaigned on the basis of holding a referendum on Scotland becoming an independent country. Held in 2014, the Scottish people voted to stay in the UK, but it had been close, and Nicola was credited with running an effective campaign.

After losing the referendum, Salmond resigned and Nicola was elected as first minister. Introducing her government, she said she would continue to push for more powers for Scotland and went on to appoint a cabinet with a fifty–fifty gender balance.

In the UK general election of 2016, Nicola led the SNP to a historic landslide victory, with the party going from six seats to fifty-six of the fifty-nine Scottish seats in Westminster. She followed this with win after win. The SNP were by far the largest party in Scotland at general elections in 2017 and 2019, and by any measure they won the Scottish elections in 2016 and 2021. Bringing the minority Green Party into government after the 2021 vote produced a parliamentary majority in favour of independence, and in 2022 Nicola set out plans for a second independence referendum.

Nicola would not see that referendum through. She made the unexpected announcement in 2023 that she was stepping down, saying she knew 'in my head and in my heart' it was the right time. The young girl who hid from attention at her birthday party was quite different from the woman who took centre stage for more than eight years as Scotland's longest-serving first minister.

'Biography: Nicola Sturgeon', Scottish Government, www.gov.scot/about/who-runs-government/first-minister/biography

Brooks, Libby, 'Nicola Sturgeon hails her appointment as positive message to girls of Scotland', *Guardian*, 19 November 2014, www.theguardian.com/politics/2014/nov/19/nicola-sturgeon-postive-message-girls-scotland-women

Friedman, Ann, 'Nicola Sturgeon', *The Gentlewoman*, Issue 15, Spring–Summer 2017, thegentlewoman.co.uk/library/nicola-sturgeon

'Nicola Sturgeon', politics.co.uk, www.politics.co.uk/reference/nicola-sturgeon-profile

'Nicola Sturgeon biography extracts: old friends and colleagues recall a talented, driven graduate', *Sunday Post*, 15 March 2015, www.sundaypost.com/politics/nicola-sturgeon-biography-extracts-old-friends-and-colleagues-recall-a-talented-driven-graduate

Rhodes, Mandy, 'Profile: Nicola Sturgeon spoke to Mandy Rhodes about her miscarriage', *Holyrood*, 5 September 2016, www.holyrood.com/inside-politics/view,profile-nicola-sturgeon-spoke-to-mandy-rhodes-about-her-miscarriage_12315.htm

Ritchie, Meabh, 'Rise of Nicola Sturgeon: from "nippy sweetie" to SNP leader?', Channel 4 News, 24 September 2014, www.channel4.com/news/sturgeon-snp-scotland-independence-campaign

The Scotsman, 'Who is Nicola Sturgeon?', Daily Motion, www.dailymotion.com/video/x7zr93t

'Who is Nicola Sturgeon? A profile of the SNP leader', BBC, 26 May 2017, www.bbc.co.uk/news/uk-scotland-25333635

Ruth Mompati

SOUTH AFRICA

*In 1994 Ruth Mompati was among the first women
elected to the first democratic South African parliament*

Ruth Mompati's role model was her grandmother, a woman who
could defend herself, entertained the family with stories and lived
to over 100. Born in 1925 in the north-west of South Africa, Ruth
and her family would rise at 5 a.m. to go to the fields to work and
'only leave when the birds had gone'. She was fourteen when her
father died so took up work to support her family, later training
as a teacher. She married in 1952 and moved to Johannesburg.
There she became active in the African National Congress (ANC),
the party dedicated to winning voting rights for Black Africans
and to eliminate apartheid, the white supremacist system of racial
segregation.

Ruth left teaching, saying there was 'no way' she would teach the
newly enforced 'Bantu education', a separate, inferior system for
Black children, teaching them manual labour and menial jobs. She
learned shorthand and began working for Oliver Tambo and Nelson
Mandela at the only Black law firm in Johannesburg. Large queues
formed outside the office but no one was turned away, even though
only about a third could pay. She became known as Mama Ruta, a
caring guardian and leader.

Ruth became prominent in the ANC, serving in multiple roles.
She was a founder member of the Federation of South African
Women and was one of the organisers of the historic women's
march in 1956. On 6 August of that year, 20,000 women of all

ethnicities demonstrated in the capital, Pretoria, against the return to pass laws (requiring Black women to carry a passbook document, just as Black men had been required to do for decades) and other increasingly repressive laws that enforced segregation. After standing in silence for thirty minutes to demonstrate non-violent dissent, they sang a protest song, 'Wathint' Abafazi, Wathint' Imbokodo', meaning 'Now you have touched the woman, you have struck a rock'. The day would be declared National Women's Day by the democratic government in 1995.

A passbook protest in 1960 in the Black township of Sharpeville became a massacre when police opened fire on the crowd. The resulting demonstrations across the country led to the apartheid government declaring a state of emergency. The ANC was banned and Ruth was instructed by the party to go underground and undergo military training. She left her small sons with her mother, hoping to return in a year. While she was gone, Mandela and the ANC leadership were arrested. As part of the armed wing of the ANC, she was told by Tambo not to return to South Africa. 'I cried about my children and my country,' she said, and took Mompati, the name of her first son, as her surname.

She worked in exile for the ANC, mobilising international solidarity. She was able to return to South Africa only in 1990, when she was part of the ANC's delegation which negotiated with the ruling National Party to end apartheid. In 1994 she was elected as a member of parliament. She then became ambassador to Switzerland and when she returned she was elected mayor of Vryburg, where she had grown up.

In 2014 the ANC presented Ruth with its highest honour, the Isithwalandwe/Seaparankoe award, meaning 'the one who wears the plumes of the rare bird'. In the words of the ANC, 'It is an award bestowed on only the bravest warriors of the people.'

'1990s: Women before and after the first democratic election', www.sahistory.org.za/sites/default/files/DBE_Booklet_5.pdf

'Dr Ruth Segomotsi Mompati', South African History Online,
www.sahistory.org.za/archive/dr-ruth-segomotsi-mompati

Joubert, Pearlie, 'The plaasjapie typist who called her boss "Nelson"',
Sunday Times, 8 December 2013, www.timeslive.co.za/sunday-times/
lifestyle/2013-12-08-the-plaasjapie-typist-who-called-her-boss-nelson

'The life of the late Dr Ruth Segomotsi Mompati', www.gov.za/sites/
default/files/speech_docs/Profile%20of%20Dr%20Ruth%20
Segomotsi%20Mompati%20.pdf

Mataboge, Mmanaledi, 'Struggle icon Ruth Mompati mothered the
movement', *Mail & Guardian*, 15 May 2015, mg.co.za/article/2015-05-
15-struggle-icon-ruth-mompati-mothered-the-movement

'Ruth Mompati', South African History Online, www.sahistory.org.za/
people/ruth-mompati

'Ruth Mompati: from typist to ambassador', eNCA, 12 May 2015,
www.enca.com/south-africa/ruth-mompati-typist-ambassador

'SACP tribute to Comrade Ruth Mompati delivered by Second Deputy
General Secretary, Comrade Solly Mapaila', Pan-African News Wire,
28 May 2015, panafricannews.blogspot.com/2015/05/sacp-tribute-
to-comrade-ruth-mompati.html

Sisulu, Elinor, 'Obituary: Dr Ruth Mompati: A brave warrior dearly
loved', news24, 17 May 2015, www.news24.com/citypress/Voices/
OBITUARY-Dr-Ruth-Mompati-A-brave-warrior-dearly-loved-20150517

Turok, Karina, *Life and Soul: Portraits of Women who Move South Africa*, South
Africa: Double Storey, 2006

Carol Martin

AUSTRALIA

In 2001 Carol Martin was the first Aboriginal
woman elected to the Australian parliament

When asked what prompted her to stand for parliament, Carol replied, 'That bloody husband of mine! It's all his fault. I blame him.' But Carol was never a person to do something she didn't want to do. Born in 1957 in Subiaco, a suburb of Perth in Western Australia, as Carol Pilkington, like a large number of Aboriginal children she was taken from home and placed in foster care at the age of twelve under a ruling which legally removed her from her family until age eighteen. Carol repeatedly ran away and at fifteen made a decision to stay with her mother in the coastal town of Broome. The local community protected her from the authorities, which she says 'changed the entire direction of my life'.

She won a scholarship to study social work and went on to see first-hand the impact of the removal of Aboriginal children. The 1981 report 'Children in Limbo' identified Aboriginal children missing in the care system and Carol worked tirelessly to return them. She said, 'I have witnessed members of the stolen generation being returned to families, children discovering they were adopted and being unable to come to terms with that realisation, and women never recovering from relinquishing their children and mourning that loss for the rest of their lives.'

In 1993 Carol joined the Australian Labor Party and became a councillor, providing her with her first political experience. Her husband Brian Martin had run for the national seat of Kimberley in 1996, missing out by a small number of votes, and realised the Labor Party would therefore not endorse him again in 2001. Carol recalled, 'He says to me, "You'll have to do it." "No way, mate, I'm not doing that; bullshit." Anyway, he said, "Ask around and see what people think." He did that and they all said, "Yeah, you should because you've got a loud mouth."'

Carol travelled 60,000 kilometres to make herself known in the remote communities across Kimberley in Western Australia. She was supported in her bid by Emily's List, the Australian network for Labor women politicians, modelled on the successful US model (founded to fund campaigns for Democratic women). She easily won the seat of Kimberley, polling 43 per cent of the vote.

In her inaugural speech Carol said, 'I have been humbled by my victory and entry into parliament. I recognise the efforts of the many people who have fought for the rights of Aboriginal people. I stand here because they never gave up their struggle. Just as I have benefited from their fight, our young people will benefit from knowing that if they believe in themselves, their law and their culture, nothing is beyond them... They are not alone; we are clearing a path for them.'

Carol's career focused on keeping Kimberley's needs on the public agenda, despite its geographic isolation, and to seek solutions to the poverty and injustice experienced by her constituents. Carol held her seat for ten years before stepping down following a bitter dispute over a constituency project for a liquefied natural gas hub, which was supported by indigenous landowners but rejected by local protest groups.

When giving her final speech in the Western Australia Legislative Assembly in 2012, she took the opportunity to call for the abolition of the department of indigenous affairs, saying, 'It provides a second class service for Aboriginal people.'

Black, David and Phillips, Harry, *Making a Difference – A Frontier of Firsts*, Parliamentary History Project, Parliament of Western Australia, 2012, www.parliament.wa.gov.au/parliament/library/MPHistoricalData.nsf/

32e457f9ba7d7c5148257b5500242416/3e74a86fd66e45f7482577
e50028a6e7/$FILE/Chapter%2045.%20Carol%20Anne%20Martin
%20Making%20a%20Difference.pdf

Centenary of Federation, *Women Shaping the Nation*, Vol. 1, 2001,
herplacemuseum.com/wp-content/uploads/2017/03/2001-Honour-
Roll-Booklet.pdf

'Indigenous MP Carol Martin to resign after "coconut" slurs', *The West Australian*, 28 September 2011, www.perthnow.com.au/news/wa/
indigenous-mp-carol-martin-to-resign-after-coconut-slurs-ng-
6763047fe0b8b6ce0da52b7fa6386e68

Martin, Carol, 'Inaugural speech', Parliament of Western Australia,
1 May 2001, www.parliament.wa.gov.au/parliament/memblist.nsf/
(MemberPics)/B646A22BA5B16DE8482569FC0024CAB8/$file/
Inaug+Martin.pdf

'Martin, Carol Anne (1957–)', The Australian Women's Register,
www.womenaustralia.info/biogs/AWE0157b.htm

Mills, Vanessa and Collins, Ben, 'Carol Martin farewells parliamentary life', ABC Local, 15 November 2012, www.abc.net.au/local/audio/
2012/11/15/3633728.htm

'Mrs Carol Anne Martin', Parliament of Western Australia',
www.parliament.wa.gov.au/parliament/library/MPHistoricalData.nsf/
(Lookup)/3E74A86FD66E45F7482577E50028A6E7?OpenDocument

Clara Campoamor

SPAIN

*In 1931 Clara Campoamor was one of the
first five women elected to the Cortes in Spain,
before Spanish women had won the right to vote*

Clara Campoamor had to work from a young age. Her father died
when she was ten, leaving her seamstress mother to support the
family. Born in Madrid in 1888, Clara first worked alongside her
mother and then for the Spanish postal service, before becoming a
typing teacher. At the same time she worked as a secretary for the
liberal newspaper *La Tribuna* and mixed with feminist activists and
suffragettes. While working multiple jobs she studied part time to
gain the qualifications needed to enter the University of Madrid.
She took a law degree and graduated when she was thirty-six,
becoming the second woman to join the Madrid Bar Association
at a time when only a small number of women gained admission
to university.

After graduating, Clara opened a law practice specialising in
defending the rights of married women and famous divorce cases.
She lectured and campaigned on women's equality, becoming
increasingly influential, but wasn't drawn to a particular political
party. In 1927 she pioneered changes to child labour laws and in
1928 was a founding member of the International Federation of
Women Lawyers.

The fall of dictator Manuel Primo de Rivera paved the way for the
declaration of the Second Republic of Spain in 1931. Legislation
allowing women to stand for the Cortes was passed, even though

they were not yet allowed to vote. Clara stood as a member of the Radical Party, which supported women's suffrage. She won her seat and became the first woman in Spain to address the assembly. She used the opportunity to demand women's suffrage, labelling women's exclusion as a contravention of the republic's democratic principles. While she had some support, she was met with hostility from Catholics, conservatives and also those on the left who feared they would lose votes to women who were influenced by the Church.

Clara was part of the group charged with writing the new constitution. She was ambitious for the document and advocated for changes to divorce, equality for children born outside of marriage, and women's suffrage. She was surprisingly successful in her arguments but was defeated on the subject of women's suffrage and it was not included. The subject would return to the Cortes for debate later that year and Clara was appalled to find that even her own party opposed it, so she fought independently. Despite a highly polarised debate, suffrage for women over the age of twenty-three was passed by 161 votes to 121 in 1931.

Clara's dedication to principle over party loyalty left her isolated and she failed to win re-election in 1933. Nevertheless, the new government made her director of social services, but she resigned when the conservatives took control of three ministries. The beginning of the civil war in 1936 left Clara in fear of her life and she quickly fled to Paris. She spent many years in Argentina after her attempts to return home were refused by the fascist Franco government. She later moved to Switzerland, where she worked as a lawyer and wrote several biographies. Under Franco, voting rights were suppressed and women were only finally able to vote again in 1977, two years after his death and five years after Clara died in Switzerland.

––––––––––––––––

'Biography of Clara Campoamor, Spanish politician', Salient Women, www.salientwomen.com/2020/06/08/biography-of-clara-campoamor-spanish-politician

'Campoamor, Clara (1888–1972)', Encyclopedia.com, www.encyclopedia.
    com/women/encyclopedias-almanacs-transcripts-and-maps/
    campoamor-clara-1888-1972
Graduates Democracy, 'She waited long enough – Clara Campoamor',
    Medium, 17 January 2017, medium.com/graduatesofdemocracy/
    she-waited-long-enough-clara-campoamor-7a0e14422314
Pérez, Janet and Ihrie, Maureen, The Feminist Encyclopedia of Spanish
    Literature: A–M, Westport: Greenwood Press, 2002
Smith, Bonnie G. (ed.), The Oxford Encyclopedia of Women in World History,
    Oxford: Oxford University Press, 2008

Kamala Harris

UNITED STATES OF AMERICA

In 2020 Kamala Harris was the first woman and first
woman of colour to be elected vice president of the USA

Kamala Harris said that during her childhood she 'had a stroller-eye view of the Civil Rights movement' in Berkeley, California, as she went with her parents to marches. She says her mother instilled in her children a pride in their Jamaican and Indian heritage, 'knowing that we would face all kinds of obstacles, but she never let us believe that anything could get in the way of our dreams'. Kamala Devi Harris was born in 1964 in Oakland, California. Her parents were both immigrants: her mother was born in India and her father in Jamaica. After they separated when she was five, Kamala and her younger sister were primarily raised by their mother, who was a bio-medical cancer research scientist.

Her mother's job meant Kamala moved to Montreal, Canada, for some of her teenage years. At thirteen she successfully organised local children to protest against rules that stopped them playing on the grass in front of their building. At her high school prom Kamala was part of a group who attended without dates so that people who had not been asked out would feel included. After high school she studied political science and economics at Howard University, a historically Black college, which she described as a formative experience. She then graduated with a law degree from Hastings College in 1989.

Kamala worked as a deputy district attorney in Oakland, pro-secuting a wide range of criminal cases – from drug trafficking to child sexual abuse – and quickly rose to become district attorney. In 2010 she ran for attorney general of California and won by a tiny margin, becoming the first woman to hold the post in that state. During this time she married lawyer Doug Emhoff and became stepmother to his two children, who she says agreed to call her 'Momala'.

A speech at the Democratic National Convention and a reputation as a rising star gave Kamala a clear path to run for the US Senate in 2016 after long-term liberal senator Barbara Boxer announced she was retiring. Kamala campaigned for increases to the minimum wage, immigration reform and education reform, and won the seat by a margin of more than two to one over her rival.

Kamala's win made her the first South Asian American in the Senate and just the second Black woman. Her profile rose as she became known for using her skills as a prosecutor to question witnesses on Senate committees.

In 2019 Kamala announced she would run for the Democratic presidential nomination for the 2020 election. Initially she was a front runner with strong debate performances, but eventually dropped out and accepted Joe Biden's invitation to become his running mate. In another first, Kamala was the first Black woman to appear on a major party's national ticket. The tumultuous election was contested by incumbent President Donald Trump, but President Joe Biden and Vice President Kamala Harris won with 51.3 per cent of the vote to Trump's 46.8 per cent. Kamala's portfolio, alongside the Covid-19 pandemic and the legislative agenda, included voting rights and immigration from Central America.

Kamala has been the 'first' in numerous roles in her career and has said she is 'determined not to be the last'.

'Kamala Harris', Britannica, www.britannica.com/biography/
    Kamala-Harris
'Kamala Harris', National Women's History Museum,
    www.womenshistory.org/education-resources/biographies/
    kamala-harris

Maranzani, Barbara, 'Inside Kamala Harris' early years and multicultural upbringing', Biography.com, 20 January 2021, www.biography.com/political-figures/kamala-harris-childhood-mother-father

Reston, Maeve, 'With Kamala Harris in for Senate bid, Tom Steyer edges closer to a run', CNN, 13 January 2015, edition.cnn.com/2015/01/12/politics/kamala-harris-california-senate/index.html

Sullivan, Kevin, '"I am who I am": Kamala Harris, daughter of Indian and Jamaican immigrants, defines herself simply as "American"', *Washington Post*, 2 February 2019, www.washingtonpost.com/politics/i-am-who-i-am-kamala-harris-daughter-of-indian-and-jamaican-immigrants-defines-herself-simply-as-american/2019/02/02/0b278536-24b7-11e9-ad53-824486280311_story.html

Walker, Nigel, *United States of America: 2020 presidential election*, House of Commons Library, 19 January 2021, researchbriefings.files.parliament.uk/documents/CBP-9115/CBP-9115.pdf

Benazir Bhutto

PAKISTAN

*In 1988 Benazir Bhutto was the first woman
to be elected prime minister of Pakistan*

Benazir Bhutto says her father, Zulfikar Ali Bhutto, impressed upon her that her privilege left her with a debt, telling her, 'You've got to come back and pay that debt by serving your people.' She was born in 1953 in Karachi to a prominent political family with scores of staff in a country blighted by poverty. Her mother was a captain in the National Guards and her father was a lawyer and politician. Despite her own independence, her mother would ask her father, 'Why do you want to educate her? No man will want to marry her.' Her father replied, 'Boys and girls are equal. I want my daughter to have the same opportunities.'

Benazir was educated at a Catholic girls' school in Karachi, where Mother Eugene taught her inspirational poetry and was influential on her thinking. At sixteen she left home to study at Harvard when students on US campuses were protesting against the Vietnam War, influencing her understanding of people power. She then studied philosophy, politics and economics at Oxford University, where she was the first woman from outside the UK to be elected president of the Oxford Union debating society.

Days after her return to Pakistan, where her father had been elected prime minister, the military seized power and he was imprisoned. In 1979 he was hanged by the military government of General Zia Ul Haq. Benazir said that during her last meeting with her father he told her she should go abroad to be free but she reached through the prison bars and told him she would continue the struggle for democracy.

In the following years Benazir was arrested many times and detained for three years. Illness followed and pressure from abroad meant she was able to leave for London, where she founded an underground organisation to resist the dictatorship. In 1986 the Zia government allowed political parties to operate again, so Benazir returned to Pakistan, where huge crowds greeted her return and she called for the resignation of General Zia.

Benazir was elected co-chair of her father's former party, the Pakistan People's Party (PPP), along with her mother. When Zia died in a plane crash, free elections were held in 1988 and the PPP won. Benazir Bhutto was just thirty-five years old and was the world's youngest prime minister. She made hunger, housing and healthcare her top priorities but had agreed not to reduce Pakistan's military budget, which meant less money for social change, and she was dismissed from office after two years. While in office for a second time in 1993, she brought electricity to the countryside and built schools, but was dismissed from office again over allegations of mismanagement and corruption. In 1999 the government was overthrown by the military and she was forced back into exile in London.

In 2007, despite death threats from Islamic extremists and government hostility, Benazir returned to Pakistan. Her victory at national elections scheduled for 2008 looked likely, but a gunman fired at her car before detonating a bomb, killing more than twenty bystanders. Benazir died from her injuries and rioting erupted throughout the country.

Benazir's legacy is complex but her struggle to defend democracy cannot be denied. She has influenced women around the world, including fellow countrywoman Malala Yousafzai.

'Benazir Bhutto', Britannica, www.britannica.com/biography/
    Benazir-Bhutto

Liswood, Laura A., *Women World Leaders: Fifteen Great Politicians Tell Their Stories*, London: Pandora, 1995

Skard, Torild, *Women of Power: Half a Century of Female Presidents and Prime Ministers Worldwide*, Bristol: Policy Press, 2014

'What it takes: Benazir Bhutto', VOA, 22 September 2017, learningenglish.voanews.com/a/what-it-takes-benazir-bhutto/3993240.html

Georgina Beyer

NEW ZEALAND

*In 1999 Georgina Beyer was the first trans woman
in the world elected to be a member of parliament*

When Georgina Beyer won her seat in the New Zealand parliament it was reported as a surprising result because her constituency of Wairarapa is a conservative rural electorate, but she modestly said of her constituents, 'It's less of a reflection on me but a wonderful reflection on them.'

Born in 1957 in Wellington, Georgina is of Māori descent and was assigned male at birth. She left school at sixteen to pursue acting and in her twenties became a part of the Wellington gay nightclub scene as a singer and drag-queen performer.

Georgina was forced out of mainstream society and said of her community, 'Many of us ended up down in the street sex industry scene, on the fringes of society, utterly marginalised. I've been bru-talised and exploited; I've been pack raped. I've had to endure that kind of thing and it either kills you or it doesn't.'

Georgina described her sex reassignment surgery in 1984 as a liberating experience. After that she forged a successful career as an actress, earning a nomination for the New Zealand film and tele-vision awards for best actress in 1987.

Georgina moved to Carterton, a farming area in the Wairarapa region of New Zealand, where she worked as a radio host and social worker aiming to improve the lives of rural children. Her activism put her on the path to politics and she was elected to the district council for the Labour Party in 1993. She was the first Māori to serve on that council and consulted with local Iwi (people) on behalf of the government for the first time in nearly 100 years. She was elected Carterton mayor in 1995, making her the first trans woman mayor in the world. She went on to win a seat in parliament and was sworn in on 10 December 1999.

In her maiden speech Georgina acknowledged her status as the first trans MP, and New Zealand's role as a world leader, saying, 'We need to acknowledge that this country of ours leads the way in so many aspects. We have led the way for women getting the vote. We have led the way in the past, and I hope we will do so again in the future in social policy and certainly in human rights.'

Georgina spent eight years in government. She was integral in passing the Prostitution Reform Bill in 2003, which decriminalised prostitution and promoted the welfare and safety of sex workers. Her speech citing her own experience of sex work was met by thunderous applause and is said to have changed three MPs' minds, securing the majority needed to pass the bill.

During her political tenure, Georgina championed LGBT+ causes, including legalising same-sex civil unions. Outside of politics, Georgina and partner Michael Hoggard danced the foxtrot on the popular New Zealand TV show *Dancing with the Stars* in 2005. After a period of serious ill health Georgina stepped back from politics, declaring, 'My faith now lies with this younger generation to stand on my shoulders, just as I stood on the shoulders of those who went before me. I've done my bit to move the needle, now it's your turn.'

Beyer, Georgina, and Casey, Cathy, *Change for the Better: The Story of Georgina Beyer As Told to Cathy Casey*, Random House New Zealand, 1999

Davis, Andrew, 'Georgina Beyer: from prostitution to parliament', *Windy City Times*, 1 October 2008, www.windycitymediagroup.com/gay/lesbian/news/ARTICLE.php?AID=19494

'Georgina Beyer', New Zealand Parliament, www.parliament.nz/en/mps-and-electorates/former-members-of-parliament/beyer-georgina

'Trailblazers: Georgina Beyer', *NZ Herald*, 16 September 2018, www.nzherald.co.nz/trailblazers/news/trailblazers-georgina-beyer/ BPF7DS2A5K2VK562AZB4XEII74

Violeta Barrios de Chamorro

NICARAGUA

In 1990 Violeta Barrios de Chamorro was the first
woman to be elected president of Nicaragua

Violeta Barrios had a secure childhood in contrast to the civil war that was raging in Nicaragua. Born in 1929 in Rivas to a wealthy cattle-ranching family, she grew up horseback riding and swimming in Lake Nicaragua. Meanwhile Anastasio Somoza rose to dictatorial power in 1936, with the intervention of the USA. Violeta was sent to a Catholic girls' school in Texas, and went on to college in Virginia but dropped out and returned to Nicaragua when her father died of lung cancer.

At nineteen she met Pedro Joaquín Chamorro, whose family published the newspaper *La Prensa*. They married and had five children and for twenty-seven years Violeta supported Pedro in his outspoken editorship of the newspaper. He campaigned against the Somoza dictatorship and was regularly imprisoned. After being accused of knowing about a plot to assassinate Somoza, Violeta and Pedro escaped by canoe across the San Juan River to Costa Rica, returning to Nicaragua only after the government declared an amnesty.

In 1978 her husband was assassinated, and his death was one of the elements that sparked a revolution, led by the Sandinista National Liberation Front, which ousted the Somoza government. Violeta was invited to join the Sandinista ruling junta in 1979–80, but became disillusioned with their increasingly authoritarian policies within a year, and went on to become their strongest opposition. She took over *La Prensa* newspaper, using it to call for a return to democracy. This led to the paper being frequently shut down, then banned until 1987.

In the early 1980s the remnants of the Somoza military were being funded by the USA and fighting erupted again in rural areas, resulting in high casualties. By the late 1980s living standards were worse than a decade before and inflation was out of control. Violeta's own family itself illustrated the deep divisions in the country: two of her children supported the Sandinistas while two opposed them. Violeta used the example of her family as being politically opposed but still able to respect and love one another as the template for her aim to unify the country.

An end to the guerrilla war was negotiated in 1989 with the condition that free elections be held in 1990. Violeta was agreed as the head of a coalition of fourteen political parties called the United National Opposition (UNO), which had little in common except the purpose of removing the Sandinistas from power. She struggled with ill health during the campaign and wrote, 'In the macho culture of my country few people believed that I, a woman and an invalid, would have the strength, energy and will to last through a punishing campaign.' Despite polls that predicted a Sandinista victory, Violeta and the UNO won with 55 per cent of the vote.

During her presidency Violeta maintained her position of con-ciliation, including an amnesty for political crimes, which included asking the National Assembly to pardon the five men accused of assassinating her husband. Her reforms ended the military draft, privatised several state-owned industries and lifted censorship. A number of Sandinistas remained in the government and conse-quently the fragile peace held under her leadership. Crucially, she was able to hand over power peacefully when her term ended in January 1997.

Boudreaux, Richard, 'The great conciliator: President Violeta Chamorro reconciled Nicaragua's warring armies. But can she deliver anything else?', *LA Times*, 6 January 1991, www.latimes.com/archives/la-xpm-1991-01-06-tm-10955-story.html

'Chamorro, Violeta (1929–)', Encyclopedia.com, www.encyclopedia.com/women/encyclopedias-almanacs-transcripts-and-maps/chamorro-violeta-1929

Garcia, Rodolfo, 'Nicaragua's president asks pardon for husband's assassins', AP, 18 August 1990, apnews.com/article/b3a721edcea4036e08d53d20090cb223

Skard, Torild, *Women of Power: Half a Century of Female Presidents and Prime Ministers Worldwide*, Bristol: Policy Press, 2014

'Violeta Barrios de Chamorro', Britannica, www.britannica.com/biography/Violeta-Barrios-de-Chamorro

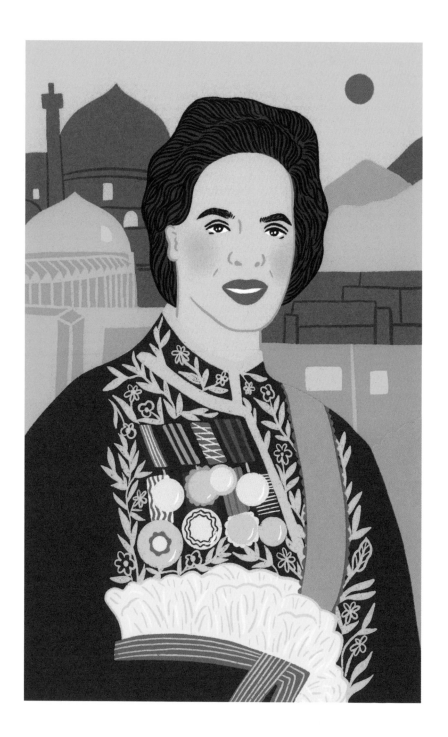

Farrokhroo Parsa

IRAN

In 1963 Farrokhroo Parsa was among the first women to be elected to parliament in Iran, and in 1968 was the first woman to become a cabinet minister

Farrokhroo Parsa was born to a mother under house arrest. It was the turn of the new year in 1922 and her mother, Fakhr Afagh, was editor of the magazine *Jahan-e Zanan* (*Women's World*). Her articles calling for equal education for girls had angered the Iranian Islamic clergy, who pressured the government to remove her from the capital, Tehran, sending the family to the city of Qom. Her mother's influence was one of the factors that would make Farrokhroo a relentless campaigner for women's rights in Iran.

When the family were able to return to Tehran, Farrokhroo was sent to school followed by college, where she earned a degree in natural sciences, becoming a biology teacher. She rose to become a school principal while also working outside of school hours to visit and teach women in prisons. She married and had four children as well as studying at the University of Tehran, graduating as a doctor in 1950.

Farrokhroo wrote to the Shah, Mohammad Reza Pahlavi, requesting votes for women and the Shah suggested he was open to the idea, writing 'my people do not consist only of men'. By 1963 the issue of women's suffrage was high on the public agenda, but the clergy objected strongly to the idea. The Shah announced a programme of reform, leading to major demonstrations equating women's franchise to prostitution. However, women's enfranchisement was made official and later that year women participated as both voters and candidates in the elections for the 21st Majles (parliament). Six women, including Farrokhroo Parsa, were elected. In office she would be a driving force for legislation for women's rights.

In 1968 Farrokhroo became minister of education, the first woman to hold a cabinet position. During her period as minister she promoted women within the ministry, ordered mixed boys' and girls' high schools to be set up in rural areas to provide girls with secondary education and oversaw the rapid growth of education to fight illiteracy. She founded several organisations during her ministry, including the Iranian Women's Organisation, the Women's House, the Women's Sports Council and the Iranian Women University Association.

The Islamic Revolution, which saw the overthrow of the Shah in 1979, led to many of the new rights for women being abolished or rolled back. Mass protests took place but women who participated, like Farrokhroo, were seen as a threat by the new Islamic republic. She lived in secret for a while but was arrested in 1980, along with her husband, and charged with 'plunder of public treasury; causing corruption and spreading prostitution in the ministry of education', among other crimes.

In her last message to her children from her prison cell, Farrokhroo wrote, 'I am not going to bow to those who expect me to express regret for fifty years of my efforts for equality between men and women.' She was executed on 8 May 1980. It was reported that several attempts to hang her failed and she was eventually shot three times. It is thought her last words were: 'The court that tried me discriminates between men and women, and I hope the future will be better for women than my lot today.'

Bahrami, Ardavan, 'A woman for all seasons', Iranian.com, 9 May 2005, www.iranian.com/ArdavanBahrami/2005/May/Parsa/index.html
'Executed but not forgotten: Iran's Farrokhroo Parsay', NPR, 23 August 2009, www.npr.org/templates/story/story.php?storyId=112150486&t =1635239126348

'Farrokhru Parsa', Abdorrahman Boroumand Center for Human Rights in Iran, www.iranrights.org/memorial/story/34914/farrokhru-parsa

'Farrokhrou Parsa's documentary on Iran's state television', Radio Zamaneh, 10 February 2013, bit.ly/3BjC3gt

'Influential Iranian women: Farrokhrou Parsa', Iran Wire, 18 May 2020, iranwire.com/fa/features/2542

Jecks, Nikki, 'I was Iran's last woman minister', BBC, 19 August 2009, news.bbc.co.uk/1/hi/world/middle_east/8207371.stm

Kilian Foerster, 'Map of the Middle East from an up-to-date Iranian textbook for 5th grade students in primary school', www.kilianfoerster.de/iran-word-4.htm

Shrivastava, Meenal and Stefanick, Lorna (eds.), *Alberta Oil and the Decline of Democracy in Canada*, Vancouver: University of British Columbia Press, 2015

Zand, Banafsheh, 'Every March 8, Iranian women stand against the regime', Alliance of Iranian Women, 8 March 2011, www.allianceof iranianwomen.org/2011/03/every-march-8-iranian-women-stand-against-the-regime

Elvia Carrillo Puerto

MEXICO

*In 1923 Elvia Carrillo Puerto was one of the first three
women to be elected to Mexico's state legislature*

Like many women who were pioneers in politics, Elvia Carrillo
Puerto was born when girls' education was in dispute, but she
experienced schooling that gave her more substance than many
girls received. She went to the first secondary school for girls in
the State of Yucatán, founded by the teacher, poet and feminist
Rita Cetina Gutiérrez, who rejected the standard girls' education of
learning domestic skills.

Elvia was born around 1881 and was raised in the small city of
Motul. She was the sixth of fourteen surviving children, and was
close to her younger brother Felipe, who would grow up to be her
trusted ally. Elvia was married at age nineteen to a local teacher but
was widowed twelve years later. She would go on to remarry un-
happily and the right to divorce became a political aim for her in
the coming years.

In 1910 Elvia was part of a rebellion which called on the
Yucatecan people to rise up in arms against the state governor.
That movement was later recognised as the first spark of the
Mexican Revolution. Elvia was part of the group of Mexican women
at the forefront of the fight and she became known as La Monja
Roja (The Red Nun). After the revolution Elvia was a founder of
the 'Feminist Resistance Leagues', which encouraged women to
organise and campaign on the right to vote, hygiene, literacy and
birth control. Organised groups were common at this time and

helped to create the socialist party for which Elvia would stand.

Tireless in her work, in 1919 Elvia created the Rita Cetina Gutiérrez League, named after her teacher and mentor. Her intention was to secure a vote on women's suffrage in Mexico City but her fellow socialists didn't share her sense of urgency. Nevertheless, her influence would find its place in her childhood ally when her brother Felipe was elected governor of Yucatán in 1922. Felipe established women's right to vote and hold office, birth control was legalised and the first legal family planning clinics were founded. Divorce was also legalised and both Felipe and Elvia were among the first to take advantage of the new law.

In 1923 Elvia was one of three women elected to the state legislature, all three of whom had been educated by Rita Cetina Gutiérrez. In office Elvia continued to work for women's advancement and land reform, but her tenure was short-lived when in 1924 Felipe was assassinated. Elvira, who tried to stay on in her elected position, was forced to leave after receiving death threats. Most reforms were rolled back and the vote for women was annulled. Elvira relocated to San Luis Potosí, where women could still stand for election, and ran for office in 1925. During the campaign, gunshots were fired at her eight times. She went on to win but the Chamber of Deputies refused to let her take her seat.

Elvia worked for women's rights the rest of her life and women in Mexico finally won the right to vote in 1953. At this time Elvia received some recognition for her work but lived largely in poverty later in life and died in Mexico City in 1968.

Boles, Janet K. and Hoeveler, Diane Long, *Historical Dictionary of Feminism*, Lanham: Scarecrow Press, 2004

Lopez, Alberto, 'Elvia Carrillo Puerto, "The Red Nun" who achieved the right to vote for women in Mexico', El País, 8 December 2017, elpais.com/internacional/2017/12/06/mexico/1512553573_210132.html

Macías, Francisco, 'The first feminist congress of Mexico', Library of Congress, 6 May 2013, blogs.loc.gov/law/2013/05/the-first-feminist-congress-of-mexico

Olcott, Jocelyn H., *Revolutionary Women in Postrevolutionary Mexico*, Durham: Duke University Press, 2006

'Recognition "Elvia Carrillo Puerto"', Senate of the Republic, www.senado.gob.mx/hoy/elvia_carrillo/biografia.php

'The Yucatán governor who empowered women', *Yucatan Times*, 8 November 2017, www.theyucatantimes.com/2017/10/the-yucatan-governor-who-empowered-women

Tsai Ing-wen

TAIWAN

In 2016 Tsai Ing-wen was the first
woman to be elected president of Taiwan

'I was not considered a kid that would be successful in my career,' Tsai Ing-wen said when recalling her childhood. As the youngest daughter of eleven children, she was expected to care for her father. Born in 1956 in the capital, Taipei City, Ing-wen spent her early years in Fangshan, a rural coastal township, and her father ran a highly successful auto repair and transport business. Her mixed ethnicity – Taiwanese mother and Hakka father – has been cited as one of the traits that helped her connect to supporters. Hakka people comprise about 15 per cent of the population of Taiwan and form the second-largest ethnic group on the island.

The family moved to the capital when Ing-wen was eleven and she spent her teens in downtown Taipei. This was followed with a string of academic achievements, first graduating from the prestigious Faculty of Law in Taiwan and then Cornell University in New York with a master's. She says it seemed like a good place for a young woman yearning for 'a revolutionary life'. She cemented her academic portfolio with a PhD in law from the London School of Economics. London left her with a slight British accent, an international perspective and new-found strength. 'It was only after studying abroad,' she said, 'that I gained the skills and confidence I have today.' Her father then 'called her home' and she returned to Taiwan to teach law.

In 1994 she entered government in a series of high-profile

policy roles. Ing-wen joined the Democratic Progressive Party (DPP) in 2004 and rose quickly to become its chair four years later. The DPP was created out of the democracy movement and has a history of seeking independence for Taiwan, therefore provoking hostility from China, which considers Taiwan part of its territory.

Despite her success on paper, Ing-wen has been described as 'a total atypical actor in the field of politics' because of her quiet demeanour, but her exterior belied a canny ability to make progress. A 2008 diplomatic dispatch from the USA summed up her style by saying, 'Her low-key personality may also disarm her competitors, who would do well not to underestimate [her].'

In 2014 Ing-wen ran for leader of the DPP while the Sunflower Student Movement was making headlines around the world for occupying Taiwan's parliament, in protest at a controversial trade deal with China. Ing-wen encouraged their participants to be absorbed into the DPP. With their support she went on to win a sweeping victory with 56.12 per cent of the vote in the January 2016 presidential election. She vowed to make Taiwan an indispensable member of the international community by stimulating the economy with initiatives in biotech, defence and green energy and also oversaw making Taiwan the first Asian society where same-sex marriage is legal.

Despite a turbulent first term, she won re-election in 2020. Her leadership through the Covid-19 pandemic was initially seen as a global model but then moved into a difficult transition of 'learning to live' with the disease.

Ing-wen is often profiled by journalists as being most at home swotting up on policy in the company of her cats, but she has said, 'People have this vision of me as a conservative person, but I'm actually quite adventurous.'

Phillips, Tom, 'Tsai Ing-wen: former professor on course to be most powerful woman in Chinese-speaking world', *Guardian*, 15 January 2016, www.theguardian.com/world/2016/jan/15/tsai-ing-wen-former-professor-on-course-to-be-most-powerful-woman-in-chinese-speaking-world

Rauhala, Emily, '"Reunification is a decision to be made by the people here": breakfast with Taiwan's Tsai Ing-Wen', *TIME*, 18 June 2015, time.com/magazine/south-pacific/3926185/june-29th-2015-vol-185-no-24-asia-south-pacific

Vanderklippe, Nathan, 'Tsai Ing-wen: Taiwan's quiet revolutionary', *Globe and Mail*, 15 January 2016, www.theglobeandmail.com/news/world/tsai-ing-wen-taiwans-quiet-revolutionary/article28215643

Xueying, Li, 'Democratic Progressive Party's Tsai Ing-wen becomes Taiwan's first woman president', *Straits Times*, 19 January 2016, www.straitstimes.com/asia/east-asia/democratic-progressive-partys-tsai-ing-wen-becomes-taiwans-first-woman-president

Mia Amor Mottley

BARBADOS

In 2018 Mia Amor Mottley was the first
woman to be elected prime minister of Barbados

As a child, Mia Amor Mottley reportedly once told a teacher that she would become the first woman prime minister of Barbados. Her foresight was surely influenced by her family record: her grandfather was the first mayor of Bridgetown, the capital of Barbados, while her father was consul-general in New York. Mia was born in 1965, just one year before Barbados gained independence from Britain. She went to preparatory school in Barbados and briefly to the United Nations International School in New York. She says she's always felt as though she's been a 'bridge' between the Bajan past and future.

Mia studied law at the London School of Economics and was called to the Bar of England and Wales, and later in Barbados. Entering politics in 1991 at the age of twenty-six, she served as a senator for the opposition for three years with the Barbados Labour Party (BLP). In 1994, following the BLP's victory in the general election, she was appointed to the ministry of education at the age of twenty-nine, becoming one of the youngest Bajans ever to be assigned a ministerial portfolio. She later became attorney general – the first woman to hold the position.

In 2018, during her election campaign to become prime minister, her political rivals made personal comments on her hair and clothes as well as misogynistic attacks on her as a single woman. An endorsement from the most famous Bajan in the world, Rihanna, led to media speculation that the music star's support had helped Mia win the election. In May 2018 she led the Barbados Labour Party to a landslide victory, winning all thirty seats in the House of Assembly and becoming prime minister.

In 2021 Mia was responsible for realising the country's long-held desire to remove the queen as head of state, and replace her with an elected president, so becoming a republic. Though she was criticised for failing to hold a referendum on the subject, she said, 'It is an assertion that it must be available to every Barbadian boy and girl to aspire to be the head of state of this nation. It is not just legal, it's also symbolic as to who or what we can become globally.'

She has become an increasingly authoritative voice on the subject of climate change despite her nation's diminutive size, arguing that islands such as those in the Caribbean are particularly vulnerable: 'We didn't cause these greenhouse gas emissions to explode through the roof, but we are on the front line of it.' She evoked US political pioneer Shirley Chisholm (see page 171) when she described her ability to intervene on behalf of small nations, saying, 'It is a folding chair that I've brought to the table.'

At the time of writing Mia had announced plans to hold a referendum on same-sex marriage and to open diplomatic missions in Ghana, Kenya, Morocco and the United Arab Emirates. She has received praise for her powerful oratory and direct way of addressing other world leaders. At the United Nations in 2021 she lit up the internet with her speech in the face of the Covid-19 pandemic, telling the assembled delegates, 'If we can find the will to send people to the moon and solve male baldness… we can solve simple problems like letting our people eat.'

'Barbados elects Mia Mottley as first woman PM', BBC, 25 May 2018, www.bbc.co.uk/news/world-latin-america-44254140

'Barbados's mucky election', *Economist*, 24 May 2018, www.economist. com/the-americas/2018/05/24/barbadoss-mucky-election

'Barbados Prime Minister Mia Mottley makes headlines with UN speech that quoted Bob Marley', Jamaicans.com, jamaicans.com/barbados-prime-minister-mia-mottley-makes-headlines-with-un-speech-that-quoted-bob-marley

'Mia Amor Mottley', Caribbean Elections, caribbeanelections.com/knowledge/biography/bios/mottley_mia.asp

'Prime Minister of Barbados – The Honourable Mia Amor Mottley, Q.C., M.P.', Barbados.org, barbados.org/people/mia-mottley.htm#.YYVtANbP1QI

Younge, Gary, '"It didn't stop Rihanna…": History-making Prime Minister Mia Mottley has monumental plans for Barbados', *British Vogue*, September 2021, www.vogue.co.uk/arts-and-lifestyle/article/mia-mottley

Constance Markievicz

IRELAND

*In 1918 Constance Markievicz was the first woman elected to the British
parliament, and was the only woman to serve in the first Dáil Éireann*

Constance Georgine Gore-Booth came from an aristocratic
Anglo-Irish family and was the first of five children of Georgina
and Henry Gore-Booth, 5th Baronet of Sligo. Born in 1868, she had
a privileged upbringing in County Sligo in the north-west of the
island of Ireland, where she learned to ride and sail while being
educated at home. When she was nineteen she went to London
for the social season. As a new socialite she was expected to find
a husband, but she persuaded her parents to allow her to enrol at
the Slade School of Art, where she joined the National Union of
Women's Suffrage.

Constance then moved to Paris to study, where she met and
married the Polish artist Count Casimir Dunin-Markievicz, becoming a countess. Settling in Dublin, Constance became a landscape
painter, but her interest in nationalist politics was growing and
she joined the revolutionary women's group Daughters of Ireland
and republican party Sinn Féin. In 1909 she split amicably from
her husband. She devoted her time to nationalist causes, including forming Soldiers of Ireland, a republican organisation loosely
based on the Boy Scouts.

In 1911 she was arrested for the first time for demonstrating against King George V's visit to Ireland. The rest of her life
would be marked by political activism and imprisonment. During
the 1916 Easter Rising, an armed insurrection against the British

135

government in Ireland, she was second-in-command of a troop of Citizen Army combatants at St Stephen's Green in Dublin. The rebels surrendered after a week and reports said that Constance kissed her revolver before handing it over to the British. She was the only woman to be court-martialled and was sentenced to 'death by being shot'. This was commuted to life in prison on account of her sex, but she was freed after just over a year under a general amnesty.

Constance was then elected to Sinn Féin's executive board, but it would not be long before she was back in prison, this time accused of a plot against the British government. It was while in jail that she was asked to stand as a Sinn Féin candidate at the forthcoming British general election. Constance was elected in 1918 while she was still in Holloway Prison. Seventeen women stood as candidates, but she was the only one to win. However, MPs had to swear an oath of allegiance to the king, which was unthinkable for members of Sinn Féin, so Constance never took her seat in Westminster. Instead the Irish republicans set up their own provisional government, the first Dáil Éireann.

On her release from prison in 1919, Constance returned to Ireland and took up membership of the Dáil Éireann, going on to become Ireland's, and indeed Europe's, first woman cabinet minister, serving as minister for labour. She was in and out of prison and elected twice more, but was eventually forced into hiding while former comrades became embroiled in the civil war.

She won a seat at the 1927 election as a founding member of the new republican party Fianna Fáil but her health was poor. She gave her money away to charitable causes, declared herself a pauper and died that year. Thousands lined the streets on the day of her funeral, and the future president of Ireland, Éamon de Valera, gave the eulogy. He said: 'The friend of the toiler, the lover of the poor. Ease and station she put aside and took the hard way of service with the weak and downtrodden.'

Arrington, Lauren, 'Constance Markievicz, the divisive revolutionary heroine', *Irish Times*, 10 December 2018, www.irishtimes.com/culture/

heritage/constance-markievicz-the-divisive-revolutionary-heroine-
1.3710763

Cafolla, Anna, 'The forgotten history of Constance Markevicz, the first
female MP', *New Statesman*, 6 January 2020, www.newstatesman.com/
politics/uk-politics/2020/01/forgotten-history-constance-
markievicz-first-female-mp

'Constance Markievicz', Britannica, www.britannica.com/biography/
Constance-Markievicz

'Countess Constance Markievicz', BBC, 24 September 2014,
www.bbc.co.uk/history/british/easterrising/profiles/po10.shtml

'The eligibility of Constance Markievicz', The History of Parliament,
thehistoryofparliament.wordpress.com/2015/12/14/the-eligibility-of-
constance-markievicz

Murphy, Eamon, 'Constance Markievicz funeral oration delivered by
Eamon de Valera', The History of Na Fianna Éireann, 17 July 2016,
fiannaeireannhistory.wordpress.com/2016/07/17/constance-
markievicz-funeral-oration-delivered-by-eamon-de-valera

Ethel Blondin-Andrew

CANADA

*In 1988 Ethel Blondin-Andrew was the first Indigenous
woman to be elected to the Canadian parliament, and in
1993 was the first woman to become a cabinet minister*

Reflecting on her life in 2019, Ethel Blondin-Andrew said, 'All of
my life I have been underestimated. I was never seen as one who
would be "most likely to succeed", even though people swear on
stacks of Bibles that they always thought I'd be a roaring success. I
don't think so! I don't remember that. I remember the challenges,
the criticism and feeling put down, but it's been my strength. It
gives you something to prove.'

Ethel was born to a Mountain Dene family, an Indigenous First
Nation people, in the Northwest Territories of Canada in 1951. Of
her childhood she said her family taught her 'to love and respect
the land, animals and the people'. She was raised on the land, travelling by dog team, boat and foot. In 1959 Ethel was sent north
by freighter plane to a residential Roman Catholic school for
Indigenous children. The Canadian residential school system isolated children from their families and culture, and the history of
terrible abuses suffered in the institutions is still being uncovered.
Ethel ran away from her school to live in a 'tent town' with other
escaped children. She said as a Dene girl she was used to tent living,
but after a few months she managed to find her way to her family
and her parents then decided 'I wasn't going to go back'.

Ethel had ongoing medical problems resulting in surgery on her
back and then a diagnosis of tuberculosis at age twelve; she used

her long recovery time to learn embroidery. When she returned to school, she was chosen for a leadership programme at a college for promising students. She says the school shaped who she became with its ethos of academic training and leadership development. Ethel went on to the University of Alberta in 1974, gaining a degree in education specialising in linguistics. This was alongside being an unmarried mother of two at this time, juggling part-time jobs to support her children. Despite being pressured to put them up for adoption, she refused to do so. She then taught at several Northwest Territories communities as one of the first accredited Indigenous teachers in the North.

Her degree and her fluency in the Dene language of North Slavey led her to work as a language specialist and to become involved in policy development for the preservation of Indigenous languages and culture. By the mid-1980s Ethel was manager and then acting director of the Public Service Commission of Canada, taking her to Ottawa and then back to Yellowknife, capital of the Northwest Territories, where she was assistant deputy minister of culture and communications. She found herself repeatedly being asked to stand for election to the Territorial Council but declined.

In 1988 Ethel finally felt the time was right and moved across from the civil service to politics at federal level, and stood in the general election, funding her campaign from her own pension pot. She won the Western Arctic seat for the Liberals and delivered her first speech in Canada's House of Commons in her Dene language, providing her own interpreter. She served for seventeen years as an MP, thirteen of them in cabinet, holding her seat for five consecutive elections. She worked on constitutional and electoral reform in relation to Indigenous people and served as Secretary of State for Training and Youth and for Northern Development.

After defeat in the federal election of 2006, Ethel went on to head the organisation that oversees the land claim settlement her Dene nation signed with the federal government. Ethel regularly speaks on Indigenous conservation in the face of climate change, and on promoting the well-being of Indigenous peoples. When asked what stood out for her in her political life, she cited always making time for visitors from anywhere in Canada, because 'the way you treat people is the way that you will be remembered'.

_____

Commonwealth Secretariat, *Women in Politics: Voices from the Commonwealth*, London: Commonwealth Secretariat, 1999

'Ethel Blondin-Andrew', The Canadian Encylcopedia, last edited 4 July 2022, www.thecanadianencyclopedia.ca/en/article/ethel-blondin-andrews

Federation HSS, 'Yáázǫ Kéorat'ı̨ (We see the daylight) – The Honorable Ethel Blondin-Andrew', YouTube, 7 July 2021, www.youtube.com/watch?v=CwEA9Iyxyz0

Geddes, John, 'From residential school runaway to trailblazing MP', MacLean's, 4 December 2019, www.macleans.ca/politics/ottawa/from-residential-school-runaway-to-trailblazing-mp

'Honourable Ethel Blondin-Andrew, P.C.', Canadian Mountain Network, www.canadianmountainnetwork.ca/about/directory/honourable-ethel-blondin-andrew

'The Honourable Ethel Blondin Andrew, P.C., O.C.', Indigenous Leadership Initiative, www.ilinationhood.ca/team/ethel-blondin-andrew

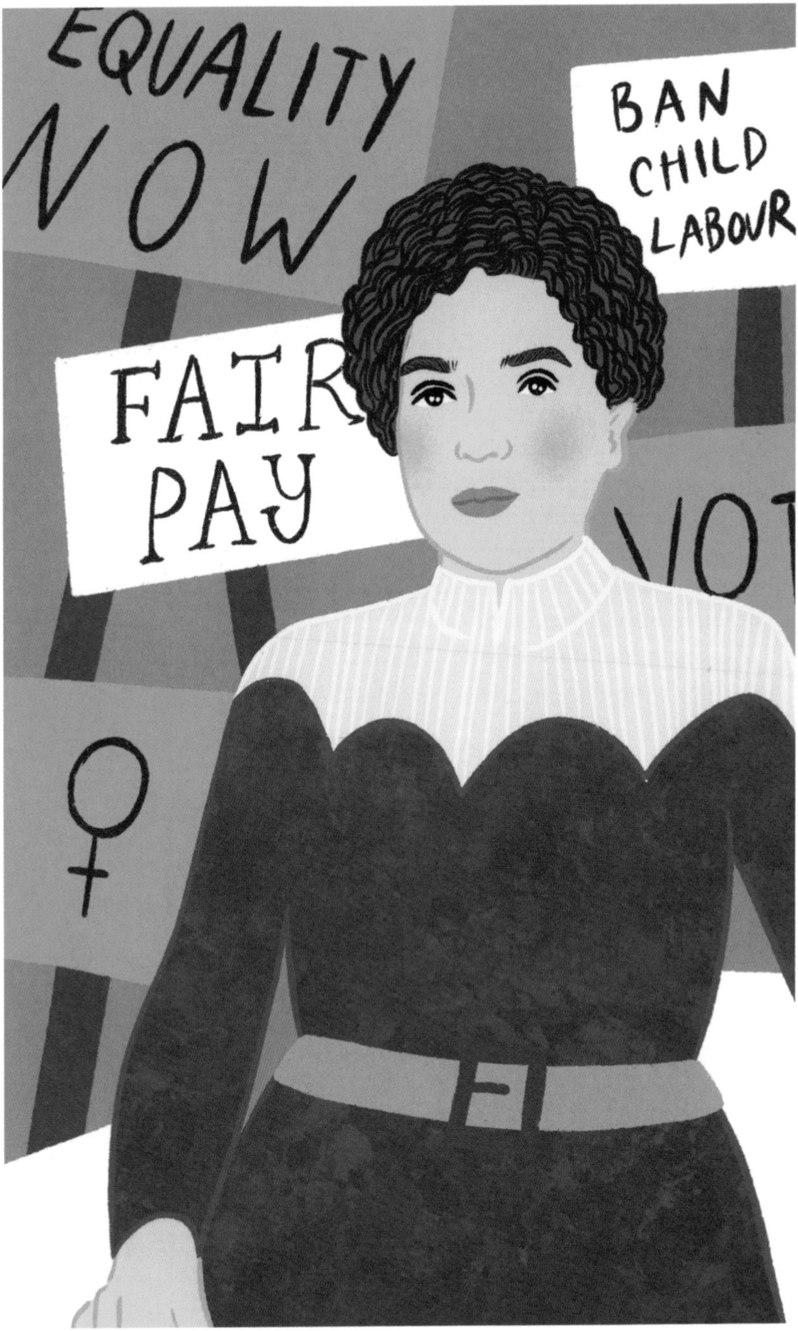
EQUALITY
NOW
BAN
CHILD
LABOUR
FAIR
PAY

Anna Boschek

AUSTRIA

*In 1919 Anna Boschek was one of the first
eight women elected to the Austrian parliament*

Anna Boschek knew more than most the personal consequences of child labour and unsafe workplaces in late nineteenth-century Europe, and she would spend her life dedicated to changing them for the better. She was the third of eight children in an impoverished household, born in Vienna in 1874. Anna had completed just four years of primary school when her father died. Without her father's wage as a railway mechanic, the family would become destitute, so she left school and worked from the age of nine.

Anna went out to factory work when she was eleven, starting in a pearl-blowing workshop, then an electroplating factory where she suffered chemical burns to her face and hands. An apprenticeship at a silver factory had to be abandoned when she developed severe eye problems. She worked in various other dangerous industry jobs for long hours and little pay, there being no child labour laws at the time. It was the solidarity of other women workers supporting her that led her to understand the value of workers banding together, and she became involved in the trade union movement and a member of the Social Democratic Party (SDP). In 1891 she discovered the SDP's educational programme and was a devoted attendee of Sunday lectures and began to gain the education she had missed out on as a younger child.

From 1894 she began to work directly for the trade union and took part in organised strikes and rallies, becoming known for her powerful speeches. She went on to become the secretary of the trade union commission and was part of a group who recruited thousands of women into the union movement and argued for their rights. Alongside this she was deeply involved in the SDP and was the first woman on the party executive committee. At the party conference in 1900 she criticised the SDP for its failure to advance women's suffrage. It would take another eighteen years for Austrian women to finally win the vote and be able to stand for election. Anna put herself forward and was elected to the National Assembly in early 1919. Able at last to use her position to bring about the changes she had campaigned for all her life, Anna and her colleagues brought in legislation on the eight-hour working day, banning child labour and the introduction of a minimum wage.

The rise of fascism in Europe would put an end to Anna's career. In 1933 the Austrian parliament was suspended and Social Democrats were expelled from politics and placed under surveillance. Anna was arrested and held in prison for seven weeks. She survived the Second World War but was not able to return to politics when democracy was reinstated in 1945. She did, however, remain a constant feature of party meetings for her entire life. At the age of eighty she was still lecturing at political training courses, and in the summer of 1957, a few months before her death, she made her last major appearance at the International Socialist Women's Conference held in Vienna.

'Anna Boschek', Republik Österreich, www.parlament.gv.at/WWER/ PAD_00155/index.shtml#

'Anna Boschek', Wien Geschichte Wiki', www.geschichtewiki.wien.gv.at/ Anna_Boschek

'Boschek, Anna (1874–1957)', Encyclopedia.com, www.encyclopedia. com/women/encyclopedias-almanacs-transcripts-and-maps/ boschek-anna-1874-1957

'Objekt des Monats März 2019: Frauen im Parlament: Anna Boschek', wienbibliothek im rathaus, www.wienbibliothek.at/bestaende-sammlungen/objekt-monats/objekte-monats-2019/objekt-monats-maerz-2019-frauen-im-0

Bidhya Devi Bhandari

NEPAL

*In 2015 Bidhya Devi Bhandari was the
first woman to serve as president of Nepal*

Bidhya Devi Bhandari cites an incident in her childhood as a formative experience. When she saw an angry mob beat and torture an elderly woman accused of being a witch, she said it motivated her to be an activist for women's rights. Bidhya was born in 1961 in Manebhanjyang in the eastern hills of Nepal to a farming family. She went to local schools and then on to higher education in Biratnagar.

In 1978 she joined the youth league of the Communist Party of Nepal (Unified Marxist–Leninist) without the knowledge of her family. 'My mother said I should stay home and not join leftist politics because the then regime was chasing and arresting the communists.' Nonetheless she joined the 1979 student movement for democracy, which was pushing the monarchy to relinquish its political power and introduce a multi-party system. This was the start of her political career as she became leader of the Eastern regional students' union. The protests ended in a referendum which led only to minor changes to the current system, and activists like Bidhya were forced underground. During this time she met Madan Bhandari, a prominent leader in the movement. They married in 1982 and had two daughters, continuing their activism together.

In 1990 democracy was reinstated in Nepal under pressure from the people's movement, and Bidhya's husband went on to lead the Communist Party to election victory in 1991. In 1993 he was killed in an unexplained road accident and Bidhya stood for his seat in the by-election that was created. She won against former prime minister Krishna Prasad Bhattarai, becoming the member of parliament for Kathmandu. At the same time she was elected as the president of the All-Nepal Women's Association, serving in both roles for three consecutive terms. In 1997 she was promoted to become minister for environment and population.

Well known for her work promoting women's rights, in 2006 she successfully introduced a policy to reserve 33 per cent of seats in the Nepali parliament for women, as well as in the state's political structures at every level. She continued to rise in status becoming the first woman to serve as defence minister in 2009 and in the same year became the party's vice chair.

In 2015 parliament elected her as Nepal's second president – a largely ceremonial role including the title of Supreme Commander of the Armed Forces. As president, she promised to champion minority and women's rights in Nepal. She was re-elected in 2018.

After her presidential election win she reflected on women's experiences in Nepal, saying, 'People still think women should only do household work. They are still mistreated, discriminated against and insulted.' When asked what difference it would make having a woman president, she said, 'The impact it makes in the mindset of people is priceless and incomparable.'

'100 women interview their president', BBC Media Action, 1 December 2015, www.bbc.co.uk/blogs/bbcmediaaction/entries/575e26d7-8988-4e24-9ae4-83813ad64109

'Bidhya Devi Bhandari elected Nepal's first female president', BBC, 29 October 2015, www.bbc.co.uk/news/world-asia-34664430

'The President', The Official Portal of Government of Nepal, nepal.gov.np:8080/NationalPortal/view-page?id=41

'Profile of Right Honourable President Bidya Devi Bhandari', Office of the President of Nepal, president.gov.np/biography-of-rt-honble-president-bidhya-devi-bhandari/

Rai, Om Astha, 'The first woman president', *Nepali Times*, 28 October 2015, archive.nepalitimes.com/blogs/thebrief/2015/10/28/the-first-woman-president

Sharma, Gopal, 'In patriarchal Nepal, first female president works for equality', Reuters, 10 November 2015, www.reuters.com/article/nepal-woman-president-idUKKCN0SZ1IR20151110

Diane Abbott

UNITED KINGDOM

*In 1987 Diane Abbott was the first Black woman
elected to the UK House of Commons*

Diane Abbott describes growing up in a tight-knit Caribbean
community in London, where she was born in 1953. Her parents
had both come from Jamaica as part of the Windrush generation,
encouraged to take up jobs to rebuild the UK after the Second World
War. The Notting Hill Race riots in 1958 happened less than a mile
away from their home and Diane recalls white racists banging on
doors looking for Black people to attack. Her parents were strongly
focused on education and her family moved to the suburbs, where
she passed the exam to go to Harrow County Grammar School,
becoming the only Black student. She recalls a teacher accusing her
of copying an essay because she couldn't believe Diane had written
it. Nonetheless she excelled and placed huge value on her education. She said, 'The thing that enabled me to go further and higher
was entirely my education. Education is a liberating force.'

Despite a lack of support from her school, Diane won a place at
Newnham College, Cambridge. She had joined the Labour Party
in 1971 and she studied history, a degree that she says enabled her
to learn about politics. She followed her degree by working at the
Home Office; when she was asked why she wanted to work there
she replied, 'Because I want power.'

In 1982 Diane was elected to Westminster City Council in the
ward where she had been born. When she stood to become MP for
Hackney North and Stoke Newington in 1987 she lacked support

from the national party. Locally some white activists refused to work with her, accusing her of being on the extreme left, but racism played a significant role, so she recruited help from local Black organisations. Bricks were thrown through her campaign office window, while the Conservatives, who had featured her on their local campaign posters as an example of 'militant Labour', had their offices firebombed. Despite this chaotic environment Diane won the seat with a healthy majority. On entering parliament she said her aim was to serve her constituents, and she became a stalwart figure on the back benches. Indeed, in addition to being the first Black woman to be elected to parliament, she is also Britain's longest-serving Black MP.

Diane had a son in 1991 and split with her husband not long afterwards, while working in a parliament that was openly hostile to family-friendly policies. She received no maternity leave and was back in parliament eight days after giving birth. She was the first person to take a baby through the voting lobby and was publicly reprimanded for it. Through the 1990s Diane increased her vote share at general elections and became a well-known and popular face on television. She founded the London Schools and the Black Child initiative to raise educational achievements among Black children and was also a vocal campaigner on human rights issues, including anti-terrorism legislation.

In 2010 she unexpectedly stood to become Labour leader, arguing that the leadership contest needed at least one runner who was not white and male. Though she didn't win, the new leader Ed Miliband promoted her to the front bench, making her shadow minister for public health. Under Jeremy Corbyn's party leadership, she served as shadow home secretary, and in 2019 she became the first Black MP to represent their party at the dispatch box during Prime Minister's Questions.

Diane is cited as a role model by many women of colour on their journey into politics in the UK. As a child, Diane had three ambitions: to be an MP, to have a family, and to write a book. She has achieved all three.

'Abbott, Diane', politis.co.uk, www.politics.co.uk/reference/diane-abbott

'Abbott, Diane 1953–', Encyclopedia.com, www.encyclopedia.com/
people/history/british-and-irish-history-biographies/diane-abbott

Beckett, Francis, 'In praise of Diane Abbott', The New European,
25 November 2021, www.theneweuropean.co.uk/in-praise-of-
diane-abbott

Bunce, Robin, *Diane Abbott: The Authorised Biography*, London: Biteback
Publishing, 2020

Bunce, Robin and Linton, Samara, 'How Diane Abbott fought racism
– and her own party – to become Britain's first black female MP',
Guardian, 29 September 2020, www.theguardian.com/politics/2020/
sep/29/how-diane-abbott-fought-racism-and-her-own-party-to-
become-britains-first-black-female-mp

Hussein-Ece, Baroness, 'Diane Abbott, The Authorised Biography: the
journey of a Black woman who defied the odds and made history',
The House, 17 October 2020, www.politicshome.com/thehouse/
article/diane-abbott-theauthorisedbiography-the-journey-of-a-
black-woman-who-defied-the-odds-and-made-history

Law, Dr Kate, 'Diane Abbott: A potted herstory of a pioneer by Drs Robin
Bunce and Samara Linton', Women's History Network, 21 October
2020, womenshistorynetwork.org/diane-abbott-a-potted-herstory-
of-a-pioneer-by-drs-robin-bunce-and-samara-linton

'Profile: Diane Abbott', BBC, 5 January 2012, www.bbc.co.uk/news/
10276583

Ribeiro-Addy MP, Bell, 'Diane Abbott MP – 33 years as a titan of
British politics', Black History Month, 18 November 2020,
www.blackhistorymonth.org.uk/article/section/bhm-firsts/
diane-abbott-mp-33-years-as-a-titan-of-british-politics

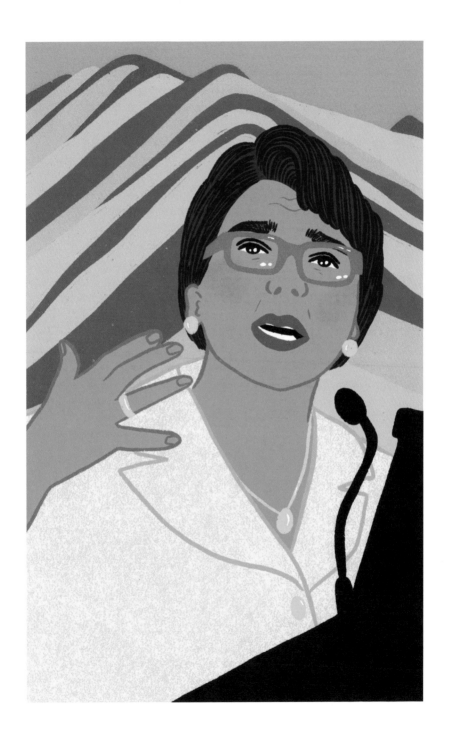

Beatriz Merino

PERU

*In 2003 Beatriz Merino was the first
woman to serve as prime minister of Peru*

'People really need to know you care for them, you work for them, and you're somebody really in touch with their souls, their pain and their desires,' said Beatriz Merino in 2019. It's a philosophy learned from her parents; she described her father as a dreamer and her mother as 'all business', and both were hugely influential on her. According to Beatriz, they instilled in her the belief that she could achieve whatever she set out to do.

Beatriz was born in Lima in 1947, where her father was treasurer of the San Isidro municipality. She studied law at the National University of San Marcos in Lima and her outstanding work won her a scholarship to the London School of Economics. She continued to excel, becoming a Fulbright scholar and the first Peruvian woman to graduate from Harvard Law School in 1977. She then worked at Proctor & Gamble as a corporate executive lawyer and only in her forties turned towards politics.

The 1980s were a turbulent time in Peru, with terrorism, hyperinflation and poverty causing misery. Beatriz met Peruvian novelist Mario Vargas Llosa at a party, and he encouraged her to stand for election. She says she decided 'it was my time, to leave all the comforts my successful career had given me and to be the change'. Beatriz was elected as a senator in 1990 but her term was cut short when President Alberto Fujimori dissolved Congress with the help of the military and suspended the constitution.

Instability followed, but a new constitution was created in 1993 and elections were held again in 1995. Beatriz stood for Congress, getting elected as an independent. She achieved what she called 'small victories', such as a bill increasing women's participation in politics and change to legislation that had allowed a rapist to go free if he married the victim.

In 2000 Beatriz ran for vice president but was defeated. President Fujimori had claimed victory in the election despite voting irregularities and resigned later that year. Fresh elections were held, and new president Alejandro Toledo inherited a country with complex problems. With national strikes, the resurgence of guerrilla forces and unemployment on the increase, President Toledo's cabinet resigned twice in two years and was in need of a new prime minister. Beatriz was proposed and she said that as a 'hard-core Catholic' she turned to God to make her decision. She accepted the role which others had feared to take in the struggling government. She was popular with the public and gave the president a boost in popularity that he badly needed.

She lasted as prime minister just under six months, facing a wave of political attacks in the press accusing her of finding jobs for friends, but also personal attacks. It was reported that the president asked her to resign because he disagreed with her decision to go public about the spreading of homophobic rumours that she was a lesbian. Peru's socially conservative Catholic culture meant the LGBT+ community faced widespread prejudice. In addition, newspapers speculated that her popularity was threatening to the president. Toledo fired her along with her cabinet.

Still a popular figure in Peru, in 2005 Beatriz was elected as Public Defender, a role dedicated to protecting constitutional rights and freedoms.

'Beatriz Merino (LLM, 1972)', London School of Economics and Political Science, www.lse.ac.uk/law/centenary/people/beatriz-merino

'Beatriz Merino Lucero', Defensoría del Pueblo, www.defensoria.gob.pe/defensores/beatriz-merino-lucero

Boustany, Nora, 'Peru's premier puts her perseverance to the test', *Washington Post*, 12 December 2003, www.washingtonpost.com/ archive/politics/2003/12/12/perus-premier-puts-her-perseverance-to-the-test/91cf40e8-c2ab-44d3-b70e-c1a4ecfaaabe

Goering, Laurie, 'Marriage option in Peru rape law is challenged', *Seattle Times*, 20 March 1997, archive.seattletimes.com/archive/?date= 19970320&slug=2529732

'An interview with prime minister Beatriz Merino of Peru', *The Henna Hundal Show*, 13 January 2019, www.thehennahundalshow.com/ episodes/2019/01/13/lessons-in-leadership-an-interview-with-prime-minister-beatriz-merino

Jensen, Jane S., *Women Political Leaders: Breaking the Highest Glass Ceiling*, London: Palgrave Macmillan, 2008

'Peru's Toledo asks cabinet to quit', *Al Jazeera*, 13 December 2003, www.aljazeera.com/news/2003/12/13/perus-toledo-asks-cabinet-to-quit

'Peruvian prime minister fired following lesbian rumor', *Advocate*, 17 December 2003, www.advocate.com/news/2003/12/17/ peruvian-prime-minister-fired-following-lesbian-rumor-10780

Hanan Ashrawi

PALESTINE

In 1996 Hanan Ashrawi was among the first
women elected to the Palestinian Legislative Council

When Hanan was a young woman, her father told her, 'Do not accept to be defined or limited by others,' and she took the advice to heart. Born to a Christian family in 1946 in Nablus, Palestine (part of the British Mandate of Palestine at that time), she was two years old when the 1948 war that established the state of Israel caused her family to flee to Jordan. They eventually settled in Ramallah, where her father was repeatedly imprisoned for his activities with the Arab Nationalist Socialist Party and the Palestinian Liberation Organisation (PLO).

Hanan was studying for her master's in literature in Beirut in Lebanon when the Six-Day War broke out in 1967 between Israel and a coalition of Arab states. The Israeli military government implemented a law defining anyone not home at the outbreak of hostilities as an 'absentee'. She found herself in exile, separated from her family, so she involved herself in organising and became spokesperson for the General Union of Palestinian Students. She said, 'You're involved in politics the moment you're born, I think, if you're a Palestinian... you don't have a choice.'

In 1973 the Israeli government allowed Palestinian exiles to re-join their families, but it was a difficult journey. Hanan, who by now had gained a PhD from the University of Virginia in the USA, was interrogated in Paris, detained in Egypt and questioned in Jordan, but finally crossed the bridge. There she established the English department at Birzeit University, joining demonstrations to protest against Israeli incursions into the campus, and was detained on many occasions. She consequently founded the Committee for Legal Aid and Human Rights.

In 1987, sustained Palestinian protest against Israel's occupation of the West Bank became the First Intifada (translated as 'to shake off'). Having worked behind the scenes, Hanan emerged into the limelight as a key negotiator. Her new international profile belied the reality of being a Palestinian from territory under occupation. When travelling abroad, she was strip-searched at airports and border crossings.

Hanan served as the official spokesperson of the Palestinian Delegation to the Middle East Peace Process from 1991 to 1993. The Oslo agreement in 1993 created a Palestinian Authority which had limited self-governance of parts of the West Bank and Gaza Strip. Hanan next founded the Palestinian Independent Commission for Citizens' Rights, set up to monitor and protect human rights in the Israeli-occupied territories.

In the Palestinian Authority's first elections in 1996, Hanan was one of the first five women to win seats. She accepted the post of minister of higher education but resigned in 1998 over political corruption and failure to implement reform plans. She then founded MIFTAH, the Palestinian Initiative for the Promotion of Global Dialogue and Democracy. In 2001 Hanan led protests in the Second Intifada and in 2005 co-founded Third Way, an alternative party to both Fatah and Hamas. She continued making history, becoming the first woman elected to the executive committee of the PLO in 2009. In 2020 she resigned, citing a need for renewal and reinvigoration by the inclusion of young people and women.

Reflecting on being a role model for women she said, 'Being the first is important because it breaks the impasse, creates precedents and encourages women in other fields, especially politics, to get involved.'

Amrani, Israel, 'MotherJones MA93: Hanan Ashrawi', MotherJones, www.motherjones.com/politics/1993/03/motherjones-ma93-hanan-ashrawi

'Ashrawi quits her P.L.O. post', *New York Times*, 11 December 1993, www.nytimes.com/1993/12/11/world/ashrawi-quits-her-plo-post.html

'Dr Hanan Ashrawi', St Antony's College, University of Oxford, www.sant.ox.ac.uk/people/hanan-ashrawi

Encyclopedia of Activism and Social Justice, London: SAGE Publications, 2007

'Hanan Ashrawi', Britannica, www.britannica.com/biography/Hanan-Ashrawi

Kuttab, Daoud, 'The many firsts of Hanan Ashrawi, one of Palestine's most notable politicians', *Arab News*, 8 March 2019, www.arabnews.com/node/1463406/middle-east

'Senior PLO official Ashrawi resigns, calls for Palestinian political reforms', Reuters, 9 December 2020, www.reuters.com/article/palestinians-ashrawi-resignation-idUSKBN28J291

Shahwan, Najla M., 'Hanan Ashrawi: Palestinian champion of women's rights', Daily Sabah, 16 March 2021, www.dailysabah.com/opinion/op-ed/hanan-ashrawi-palestinian-champion-of-womens-rights

'This Side of Peace: A Personal Account', C-SPAN, 11 May 1995, www.c-span.org/video/?65105-1/this-side-peace-personal-account

Victor, Barbara, *A Voice of Reason: Hanan Ashrawi and Peace in the Middle East*, San Diego: Harcourt Brace & Company, 1994

Jóhanna Sigurðardóttir

ICELAND

Jóhanna Sigurðardóttir was the world's first out LGBT+ head of government, and in 2009 she was the first woman to be elected prime minister of Iceland

'My time will come' has become a common catchphrase in Iceland, seen on T-shirts and posters. The words were spoken by Jóhanna Sigurðardóttir, with her fist in the air, when she narrowly lost the leadership race for the Social Democratic Party in 1994. It reflects on Jóhanna as a politician who has patience and an eye for the right moment to make a move.

Born in 1942 in Reykjavík, Jóhanna worked as a stewardess for the airline Loftleiðir Icelandic and spent nearly ten years with the company, during which she was active in the union, becoming its chair. She married and had two sons during the 1970s and moved into commercial office work, where she sat on the board of the Commercial Workers' Union.

It was these union connections that kick-started her political career, and in 1978 she was elected to the Althingi (parliament), representing Reykjavík for the Social Democrats. She very quickly established herself as a trusted politician, becoming deputy speaker in 1979, a position she would hold twice more in the coming years.

Labelled as a rising star with an unwavering passion for social justice and welfare reform, she took her first ministerial office in social affairs in 1987 and would remain in the post until 1994, earning her the nickname 'Saint Jóhanna' for her dogged defence of social causes. She rose to become vice chair of the party and then lost her bid for the leadership.

Following this setback she resigned to form her own party, National Movement, which won four seats at the next election. However, she was reconciled with former colleagues when their parties joined together, along with two smaller parties, to form a Social Democratic Alliance for the next election.

Jóhanna once again became minister for social affairs not long before the world financial crisis of 2008. As a popular and trusted political figure, she was well placed to step into the chaos that was unfolding. In 2009 Prime Minister Geir Haarde resigned following the collapse of the nation's economy, pushing it to the brink of bankruptcy. Jóhanna's Social Democratic Alliance swept to victory in a snap election. In her victory speech she told her cheering supporters, 'Our time has come,' declaring that justice and equality would be the guidelines for the new administration.

The male CEOs of the three collapsed banks were removed, thirty-six bankers were jailed and the banks were renamed and nationalised, with women as two of the new CEOs. Iceland staged one of the fastest recoveries on record, stabilising its economy while also supporting its citizens. This period came to be known as the 'women's takeover'. The changes were not limited to the financial sector, as for the first time in Iceland's history there was gender equality in the cabinet; more widely, the country regularly came in at number one on the World Economic Forum's annual Global Gender Gap Index.

Part of Iceland's swift moves towards equality included the approval of same-sex marriage. In 2010, on the first day that legislation became effective, Jóhanna Sigurðardóttir and her partner, author and playwright Jónína Leósdóttir, were married. In 2017 Jóhanna released her biography entitled *My Time*.

Carlin, John, 'A Nordic revolution: the heroines of Reykjavik', *Independent*, 20 April 2012, www.independent.co.uk/news/world/europe/a-nordic-revolution-the-heroines-of-reykjavik-7658212. html

Gunnarsson, Valur, 'Iceland to elect world's first openly gay PM', *Guardian*, 30 January 2009, www.theguardian.com/world/2009/jan/30/iceland-elects-gay-prime-minister

'Johanna Sigurdardottir', Britannica, www.britannica.com/biography/Johanna-Sigurdardottir

'Jóhanna Sigurdardóttir', LGBT History Month, lgbthistorymonth.com/sites/default/files/icon_multimedia_pdfs/2010/2010_GLBT_Bios%2027.pdf

'Johanna Sigurdardottir', outhistory, outhistory.org/items/show/1506

'Jóhanna Sigurðardóttir: "Gender equality did not fall into our laps without a struggle"', Women Political Leaders, www.womenpoliticalleaders.org/jóhanna-sigurðardóttir-gender-equality-did-not-fall-into-our-laps-without-a-struggle-1989

Lipman, Joanne, 'How Iceland's reaction to the 2008 crash made it the best place in the world to be a woman', *Insider*, 8 February 2018, www.businessinsider.com/iceland-gender-equality-2018-2?r=US&IR=T?utm_source=copy-link&utm_medium=referral&utm_content=topbar

Marsh, Stefanie, 'The first gay First Lady: the unlikely love story of Iceland's ex PM and her wife', *The Times*, 5 March 2014, www.thetimes.co.uk/article/the-first-gay-first-lady-the-unlikely-love-story-of-icelands-ex-pm-and-her-wife-p766m5fhflr

'Profile: Johanna Sigurdardottir', BBC, 2 February 2009, news.bbc.co.uk/1/hi/world/europe/7859258.stm

'"Saint Johanna": Iceland's gay feminist', Expatica, 27 April 2009, www.expatica.com/de/uncategorized/saint-johanna-icelands-gay-feminist-93294

Skard, Torild, *Women of Power: Half a Century of Female Presidents and Prime Ministers Worldwide*, Bristol: Policy Press, 2014

Stange, Mary Zeiss, Oyster, Carol K. and Sloan, Jane E. (eds.), *Encyclopedia of Women in Today's World*, US: SAGE Publications, 2011

Tan, Garyn, 'The 10 year recovery, and lessons from Iceland', Asia & the Pacific Policy Society', 15 January 2018, www.policyforum.net/10-year-recovery-lessons-iceland

Fiamē Naomi Mataʻafa

SĀMOA

*In 2021 Fiamē Naomi Mataʻafa was the first
woman elected to be prime minister of Sāmoa*

Politics was always a topic of conversation at home for Fiamē
Naomi Mataʻafa, and she says the Sāmoan habit of including children in all areas of life meant she absorbed 'the whole idea of
service' from a young age. Fiamē Naomi was born in Apia, the capital of Sāmoa, in 1957, five years before the island nation gained
independence from New Zealand. Her mother was a teacher who
would go on to be a politician while her father was a chief who
would soon become the first prime minister of Sāmoa. Her grandfather had been involved in the non-violent movement fighting for
independence. He was, she said, her 'first adult friend'.

Fiamē Naomi's mother started a banana plantation to afford
school fees, sending her to boarding school in New Zealand
when she was ten. Fiamē Naomi and her cousin were the only two
Sāmoans in the school, but she said, 'I don't think we felt alone and
frightened because, you know... I was five foot seven when I was
eleven.' Fiamē excelled at school, enjoying extracurricular activities
including debating, plays and social events.

In 1975 Fiamē Naomi's father died unexpectedly, leaving his
title of 'Fiamē' open to extended family. Twenty-one candidates
argued for the title in court but Fiamē Naomi won, which was
seen as highly unexpected. She had been studying politics in New
Zealand, and returned there only to be challenged again in court
by family members as an 'absentee Matai' (Sāmoan chief). The

judges summarised: 'She is only twenty years old, she seems overly influenced by her mother, she is female and she is unmarried.' Nevertheless she challenged their arguments and kept her title. Fiamē Naomi says she took on board the message to come home to her community, working on educational projects and becoming a deacon of her church.

Wanting to expand her leadership duties, Fiamē Naomi stood for parliament at the age of twenty-seven and was elected. As part of the ruling Human Rights Protection Party (HRPP), she served as the country's first woman cabinet minister and the first woman deputy prime minister. However, she started to distance herself from what she saw as a declining respect for the rule of law. In 2020 she resigned in protest at legislation which she said would result in the 'destruction of the court system'.

During the 2021 election campaign Fiamē Naomi invited people into her home and travelled the country to talk with voters. Her new FAST party (whose name translates as 'Sāmoa United in Faith') and the incumbent HRPP won twenty-five seats each. One independent MP held the balance of power and agreed to support FAST, so Fiamē Naomi claimed victory, but the election was contested. An election re-run was called, but five days before the voters went back to the polls the country's supreme court validated Fiamē Naomi's victory.

She said there was 'a lot of excitement' among women and girls in the Pacific area, which has the lowest rate of female political representation anywhere in the world. She said her agenda was to make a much greater investment in the people and communities of Sāmoa. At the time of writing, Fiamē Naomi is still one of the longest-standing members of the Sāmoan parliament.

'Afioga Fiame Naomi Mata'afa', NZIIA, pacificfutures.nz/page/hon-afioga-fiame-naomi-mataafa.aspx..aspx

'Fiame to lead Samoa's FAST party', RNZ, 9 March 2021, www.rnz.co.nz/international/pacific-news/437992/fiame-to-lead-samoa-s-fast-party

Hollingsworth, Julia, 'The incredible rise of Samoa's first female Prime Minister-elect, and the man still standing in her way', CNN, 29 May 2021, edition.cnn.com/2021/05/29/asia/samoa-prime-minister-intl-hnk-dst/index.html

'Hon. Fiame Naomi Mata'afa', RNZ, www.rnz.co.nz/collections/nff-women/naomi-mataafa

Jackson, Lagipoiva Cherelle and Vai, Maina, '"Women have not been able to hold these positions": Samoa's first female PM gets down to the job', Guardian, 30 July 2021, www.theguardian.com/world/2021/jul/30/women-have-not-been-able-hold-these-position-samoas-first-female-pm-gets-down-to-the-job

O'Brien, Patricia A., 'Samoa's first female leader has made history – now she faces a challenging future at home and abroad', The Conversation, 28 July 2021, theconversation.com/samoas-first-female-leader-has-made-history-now-she-faces-a-challenging-future-at-home-and-abroad-165083

'The woman who unseated Samoa's prime minister of 20 years', BBC, 18 May 2021, www.bbc.co.uk/news/world-asia-56811379

Shirley Chisholm

UNITED STATES OF AMERICA

In 1968 Shirley Chisholm was the first Black woman elected to the
US Congress, and in 1972 she was the first woman and the first Black
candidate to seek the presidential nomination from one of the major parties

'When I die, I want to be remembered as a woman who lived in the twentieth century and who dared to be a catalyst of change,' said Shirley Chisholm of her legacy. No one could deny that Shirley more than fulfilled that role. She was the eldest of four daughters, born in 1924 in Brooklyn, New York, to a seamstress mother from Barbados and a factory worker father from Guyana. She spent her early years with her grandmother in Barbados, where she started school. Returning to New York, she excelled at high school and won scholarships to several colleges but was unable to afford the costs, so lived at home and attended Brooklyn College.

On campus she became interested in politics and was active in the National Association for the Advancement of Colored People (NAACP), and the Democratic Party club. She won prizes on the debate team but was frustrated by the lack of opportunity for women. She said women did the majority of fundraising but when they dared to say they wanted to stand for election, 'it never happened'.

In 1949 she married Conrad Q. Chisholm, a private investigator, and initially she worked as a nursery school teacher, then as the director of two day-care centres. She earned a master's degree in early childhood education and was a consultant to the New York City Division of Day Care.

In 1964, with the civil rights movement in full swing, Shirley ran for, and won, a seat in the New York State Legislature, campaigning from a truck which announced, 'Ladies and Gentlemen... this is fighting Shirley Chisholm coming through.' In 1968 she won a seat in Congress, winning soundly against civil rights activist James Farmer, who she said had laughed when he heard she was running. She kept her seat for fourteen years.

She worked on successful legislation, including the minimum wage, and was a vocal champion of poverty alleviation and opposition to the Vietnam War. She was heavily involved in the women's movement and was a co-founder of the National Women's Political Caucus in 1971, recently immortalised in the TV series *Mrs America*.

In 1972 Shirley decided to run for the Democratic Party presidential nomination. She said she felt the time had come when 'not only white males' should run 'and somebody had to get it started'. She says the moment she made the announcement 'all hell broke loose'. Shirley took legal action when she was prevented from being in the televised debates and those she might have expected to support her such as the Congressional Black Caucus were not on her side. Her campaign poster bore the slogan 'Unbought and Unbossed' to express that she had no big funders and was beholden to no one. She entered twelve primaries and won 10 per cent of the votes.

Shirley retired from Congress in 1983 but campaigned for Jesse Jackson's presidential bids in 1984 and 1988 and taught as a professor of political science. An undisputed champion of changing the status quo, her most famous advice was 'If they don't give you a seat at the table, bring a folding chair.'

Center for American Women and Politics, 'Conversation with Shirley A. Chisholm (Talking Leadership series)', YouTube, 19 December 2014, www.youtube.com/watch?v=bQPc8EMNFXE

'Chisholm, Shirley Anita', United States House of Representatives, history.house.gov/People/Listing/C/CHISHOLM,-Shirley-Anita-(C000371)/

Cullen-DuPont, Kathryn, *Encyclopedia of Women's History in America*, New York: Facts On File, Inc., 2014

Foli, Kwesi, 'Shirley Chisholm's "Unbought and Unbossed" presidential campaign poster', Andscape, 25 January 2017, andscape.com/features/shirley-chisholm-unbought-and-unbossed-presidential-campaign-poster-cover-stories

Michals, Debra, 'Shirley Chisholm', National Women's History Museum, www.womenshistory.org/education-resources/biographies/shirley-chisholm

'Shirley Chisholm Biography', Encyclopedia of World Biography, www.notablebiographies.com/Ch-Co/Chisholm-Shirley.html

The Shirley Chisholm Project, chisholmproject.com/2020/news/5082

Williams, Brenna, '#TBT: Shirley Chisholm, "a woman who fought for change"', CNN, 9 February 2017, edition.cnn.com/2017/02/09/politics/tbt-shirley-chisholm-black-history-month/index.html

Margaret Thatcher

UNITED KINGDOM

In 1979 Margaret Thatcher was the first woman
to be elected prime minister of the United Kingdom

Even today any woman who becomes a world leader and presents a tough image is likely to be compared to Margaret Thatcher. Her status as the most visible and powerful woman in world politics towers over the twentieth century and she still attracts strong feelings of admiration or anger.

Margaret was born in Grantham in Lincolnshire in 1925 where her family lived above her father's grocery shop. Her father supported the Conservative Party and Margaret was an errand girl for their parliamentary candidate when she was ten. Excelling at school, she went to Oxford to study chemistry, joining the university Conservative Association and becoming its president. She worked as a research chemist while maintaining party activities and twice ran for parliamentary seats in 1950 and 1951, losing both.

She met businessman Denis Thatcher at a political meeting, and they married in 1951 and had twins. She had by that time been studying law and applied for her final Bar exams from the maternity ward. Constituency associations were then even more reluctant to offer her a seat to stand in because they believed that a mother wouldn't have the time to commit to the role. She was finally elected to the seat of Finchley in 1959 and worked long hours, becoming a shadow minister with various portfolios. When the Conservatives won the 1970 general election, she was made secretary of state for education and became controversial for cancelling free milk for schoolchildren over the age of seven to reserve the money for the main education budget.

When the Conservatives lost the 1974 election, she was frustrated with the leadership, so stood for leader and won in 1975. The surprise at her win was palpable. In the press conference after her victory, a journalist asked, 'Are you surprised, Mrs Thatcher, that the male-dominated Parliamentary Party have elected you?' Her response: 'No, they seem to like ladies.'

On the promise of regenerating the economy, she took her party to victory in the 1979 general election. Margaret's programme of work was based on reducing spending and regulation, lowering taxes for business, curbing the power of unions and privatising publicly owned industries. Unemployment was high and her spending cuts pointed to a short term in power. However, when Argentina invaded the Falkland Islands (a British overseas territory in the South Atlantic Ocean) her determination to defend the islands cemented her reputation as the 'Iron Lady'. She formed a strong alliance with Republican US President Ronald Reagan, who shared many of her free-market impulses, and they appeared to stride the world.

She won a second term in 1983, and her government's response to the 1984–5 coal miners' strike, never meeting their demands, seriously weakened the power of the trade unions. An improving economy accompanied her third election win in 1987 but by 1990 recession was looming again. Margaret's hugely unpopular poll tax led to demonstrations and rioting, and this, along with her position on the European Union, led to her being challenged for leadership of the party from the inside. She resigned in 1990 having deindustrialised and privatised the UK beyond recognition of its post-war period.

After stepping down from the Commons, she became a member of the House of Lords and created the Thatcher Foundation to promote her ideas 'of political and economic freedom' around the world. She died in 2013.

Kennedy, Lesley, 'How the Falklands War cemented Margaret Thatcher's reputation as the "Iron Lady"', History.com, 13 November 2020, www.history.com/news/margaret-thatcher-falklands-war

Liswood, Laura A., *Women World Leaders: Fifteen Great Politicians Tell Their Stories*, London: Pandora, 1995

'Margaret Thatcher: A biography', Churchill Archives Centre, archives. chu.cam.ac.uk/collections/thatcher-papers/thatcher-biography

'Margaret Thatcher: Grocer's girl who grew up to become the Iron Lady', *Evening Standard*, 8 April 2013, www.standard.co.uk/news/uk/margaret-thatcher-grocer-s-girl-who-grew-up-to-become-the-iron-lady-8564741.html

'Press conference after winning Conservative leadership (Conservative Central Office)', BBC Sound Archive: OUP transcript, Margaret Thatcher Foundation, 11 February 1975, www.margaretthatcher.org/document/102487

Skard, Torild, *Women of Power: Half a Century of Female Presidents and Prime Ministers Worldwide*, Bristol: Policy Press, 2014

Woods, Judith, 'Margaret Thatcher: "Yes, I wish I saw more of my children. But I can't regret"', *Telegraph*, 9 April 2013, www.telegraph.co.uk/news/politics/margaret-thatcher/9982157/Margaret-Thatcher-Yes-I-wish-I-saw-more-of-my-children.-But-I-cant-regret.html

Megawati Sukarnoputri

INDONESIA

*In 2001 Megawati Sukarnoputri was the first
woman to serve as president of Indonesia*

Born in 1947, Megawati Sukarnoputri literally grew up around
politics – she spent her early years in the presidential palace. Her
father, Sukarno, was the leader of the Indonesian independence
movement and first president of Indonesia, and her name means
'daughter of Sukarno'. This could have made her political rise seem
inevitable, but that was far from the case. Her mother was Sukarno's
third wife and was outraged by his intention to marry again under
polygamy laws. She moved her family out of the presidential palace
in 1953, but kept the title of First Lady.

Pursuing an interest in gardening, Megawati went to Padjadjaran
University to study agriculture, but dropped out in 1967 after her
father fell from power, ousted by General Suharto's military government. It was understood her family had to stay out of politics if
they wanted to remain in the country.

In the 1970s Megawati married three times. Her first husband
was killed in a plane crash in 1970. She married again and the
marriage was annulled shortly after. In 1973 she married Taufiq
Kiemas, with whom she had three children. She remained at a distance from politics until a resurgent interest in her father's legacy
in the 1980s inspired her to join the Indonesian Democratic Party
(PDI) and she quickly became a popular figure in the movement.

Megawati was elected to the People's Consultative Assembly
(the legislative branch of the national parliament). As she gained

in stature and popularity, the Suharto government prevented her being elected head of the PDI to ensure she couldn't run in the 1998 presidential elections. Protests by her supporters in Jakarta led to a harsh government crackdown, resulting in riots across the capital.

Suharto resigned from office in 1998, allowing Megawati and her supporters to form the new Indonesian Democratic Party for Struggle (PDI-P), which went on to take 34 per cent of the vote in the 1999 parliamentary elections, giving them the largest number of seats in the legislature. The way seemed clear for Megawati to take the presidency but there was heavy opposition from groups such as the United Development Party. Their youth wing had campaigned with the slogan 'A Woman President? No Way'. The People's Consultative Assembly chose Abdurrahman Wahid of the National Awakening Party as president, with Megawati as vice president. After he was heavily criticised in his role, the Assembly removed Wahid from office in 2001 and named Megawati as president. She was the first woman to hold the post and the first Indonesian leader born after independence. She continued to face sexist treatment and quipped, 'It appears that I am considered to be a housewife. I say to those people who belittle housewives: What's wrong with that? It does not mean a housewife does not understand politics.'

In her three years in power the country's economy saw some improvement but she was criticised for having a hands-off approach to dealing with political corruption, unemployment and threats from Islamic militants. However, she was praised for bringing political stability to Indonesia and enabling the continuation of democracy, which is no small feat. Her brother Guntur, a former MP, asserted, 'We are not cut out for politics. It's Mega who has staying power. She has guts.'

Haeri, Shahla, *The Unforgettable Queens of Islam: Succession, Authority, Gender*, Cambridge: Cambridge University Press, 2020

'Indonesia's leading lady', BBC, 9 August 2001, www.bbc.co.uk/ worldservice/people/highlights/010809_megawati.shtml

'Megawati Sukarnoputri', 100 Women Encyclopaedia Britannica, www.britannica.com/explore/100women/profiles/megawati-sukarnoputri

'Megawati Sukarnoputri', Alchetron, alchetron.com/Megawati-Sukarnoputri

'Megawati Sukarnoputri', New World Encyclopedia, www.newworld encyclopedia.org/entry/Megawati_Sukarnoputri

'Megawati Sukarnoputri', Oxford Reference, www.oxfordreference.com/ view/10.1093/oi/authority.20110803100541365

'Megawati Sukarnoputri: The founding father's daughter, a presidency of her own', Friedrich Naumann Foundation, 13 March 2019, www.freiheit.org/sudost-und-ostasien/megawati-sukarnoputri-founding-fathers-daughter-presidency-her-own

Sahle-Work Zewde

ETHIOPIA

In 2018 Sahle-Work Zewde was the first
woman to serve as president of Ethiopia

'I had a very amazing family, especially my father, who has always told us that there is nothing that a woman or a girl cannot do. So this has been my motto all my life and in whatever I did, by the way, I was the first woman to do this, the first woman to do that, so I was daring. I was courageous and I had my self-esteem as well.' So said Sahle-Work Zewde, reflecting on her upbringing. She was born in Addis Ababa, the capital of Ethiopia, in 1950. Her father was a senior officer in the imperial army, and she was the eldest of four girls in a family that had high expectations for her.

Having graduated from the French international school in Addis Ababa, at seventeen Sahle-Work won a scholarship to attend university in France, where she studied natural science. After nine years, she returned to Ethiopia to work at the ministry of education, starting as a public relations officer and rising to head the department. She next joined the ministry of foreign affairs, becoming Ethiopia's ambassador to Senegal, then Djibouti. Contemplating what she learned from that time, she said, 'When the government appointed me to Djibouti, I was very reluctant to accept it. I thought being a woman in a Muslim country might not be conducive to getting the two countries closer. I thank the then foreign minister who insisted for me to take the position... I try to do the same for others.' Her profile continued to rise and she went on to become ambassador to France as well as becoming permanent representative to the United Nations Educational, Scientific and Cultural Organization.

Her international reputation continued to be recognised through a series of roles at the UN. She was director-general of the United Nations Office at Nairobi and in 2018 UN secretary-general António Guterres appointed her under-secretary-general, as special representative to the African Union and head of the United Nations Office to the African Union. She was the first woman to hold the position.

In 2018 Sahle-Work was unanimously elected by the Ethiopian parliament to be president of Ethiopia, replacing Mulatu Teshome, who resigned unexpectedly. In the Ethiopian constitution the post of president is ceremonial, with the prime minister holding the political power. However, her appointment was seen as significant and part of a tranche of reforms in the traditionally conservative country by Prime Minister Abiy Ahmed. Sahle-Work was elected to the position one week after the prime minister appointed a cabinet with women taking half the posts. The prime minister's chief of staff tweeted that 'in a patriarchal society such as ours, the appointment of a female head of state not only sets the standard for the future but also normalises women as decision-makers in public life'.

Sahle-Work reinforced this position, declaring that by electing a woman president 'you open the door for a better understanding, a better involvement, of gender issues'. In her first address to parliament, Sahle-Work promised to be a voice for women and stressed the importance of unity. She told MPs that if they thought she was talking too much about women, she had only just begun.

Abate, Solomon, 'Ethiopian president: "There is nothing that a woman or a girl cannot do"', VOA, 28 September 2019, www.voanews.com/a/ africa_ethiopian-president-there-nothing-woman-or-girl-cannot-do/ 6176652.html

'Celebrating Ethiopian Women: Ambassador Sahle-work Zewde', The Official Blog of MFA Ethiopia, 22 March 2018, mfaethiopiablog.

wordpress.com/2018/03/22/celebrating-ethiopian-women-ambassador-sahle-work-zewde

Gebreselassie, Elias, 'Who is Sahle-Work Zewde, Ethiopia's first female president?', Al Jazeera, 27 October 2018, www.aljazeera.com/news/2018/10/27/who-is-sahle-work-zewde-ethiopias-first-female-president

'Ms. Sahle-Work Zewde of Ethiopia – Special Representative to the African Union and Head of the United Nations Office to the African Union (UNOAU)', United Nations, 27 June 2018, www.un.org/sg/en/content/sg/personnel-appointments/2018-06-27/ms-sahle-work-zewde-ethiopia-special-representative

SABC News, 'Ethiopia will work hard to maintain peace: Sahle-Work Zewde', YouTube, 8 November 2018, www.youtube.com/watch?v=G3PpPzsFE2M

'Sahle-Work Zewde becomes Ethiopia's first female president', BBC, 25 October 2018, www.bbc.co.uk/news/world-africa-45976620

Young, Annette, 'Ethiopia's gender revolution: President Sahle-Work Zewde speaks to FRANCE 24', France 24, 30 October 2019, www.france24.com/en/africa/20191030-ethiopia-s-gender-revolution-president-sahle-work-zewde-speaks-to-france-24-1

Tina Anselmi

ITALY

In 1976 Tina Anselmi was the first woman
to serve as a cabinet minister in Italy

Born in 1927 in Castelfranco Veneto in northern Italy, Tina Anselmi's childhood was coloured by the dangers of living in a one-party dictatorship under Mussolini's National Fascist Party and during the Second World War. Her father was persecuted by Mussolini's supporters for expressing views contrary to the regime's ideology. She also experienced early grief when her younger brother disappeared when he was only twelve.

In 1943 German forces had occupied Italy and set up a puppet state led by Mussolini. Tina was seventeen when Nazi–Fascist soldiers forced her and other students at her teacher-training college to witness the hanging of thirty-one partisan prisoners, many of them not much older than her. Partisans were anti-fascists fighting a war of resistance against the state. This scene of brutality was intended to instil fear in the young people but had the opposite effect on Tina: she joined the resistance movement. Working under the assumed name 'Gabriella', she became a courier making journeys by bicycle of up to seventy miles a day, delivering messages, arms and ammunition. It was extremely dangerous work and she had seen first-hand what the consequences would be if she was caught. She later received the Italian Knight's Grand Cross for valour for her contribution.

These experiences led her towards politics and in 1944 she joined the Christian Democracy Party. She said, 'The greatest discovery I made in those months of struggle was the importance of participation. To change the world you had to be there... without participation there is no democracy and the country could go into disarray again.'

Following the war, Tina worked in primary schools, dedicating herself to union organising and party work and rising through the ranks. She was the director of the young Christian Democrats, vice president of the European Women's Union and later deputy leader of the Christian Democracy Party. She was elected a member of the Italian Chamber of Deputies in 1968 and remained an MP until 1992, re-elected five times.

In 1976 she was appointed as minister for labour and brought in legislation on equal pay and opportunities and a bill affirming the responsibility of fathers as caregivers. As minister for health she legalised abortion in the first trimester and contributed to reforms which introduced a national health service. In 1981 she presided over an inquiry into the P2 (Propaganda Due) illegal Masonic lodge, which was seen as a danger to democracy in pursuing a far-right agenda. Her pursuit of truth put her in peril: she was followed and threatened, and dynamite was left at her house. Her four-year inquiry uncovered a clear threat to power from the organisation; her recommendations were not implemented, but her work moved the country towards a closer examination of political corruption.

Tina was proposed as a potential candidate for the presidency many times, even after her retirement. Hugely respected, she is particularly remembered for her work on equal opportunities. She said, 'Women must learn to be there wherever there are problems to be tackled, because I believe that the quality of politics would be better if there were more women doing it.' She died in 2016 at the age of eighty-nine.

'Anselmi, Tina (1927–)', Encyclopedia.com, www.encyclopedia.com/women/encyclopedias-almanacs-transcripts-and-maps/anselmi-tina-1927

Di Caro, Eliana, 'Ada Gobetti e Tina Anselmi, lezioni di democrazia per i più piccoli', Isole 24 Ore, 12 April 2019, www.ilsole24ore.com/art/ ada-gobetti-e-tina-anselmi-lezioni-democrazia-i-piu-piccoli-ABJRwwjB

'Morta Tina Anselmi, prima donna ministro', adnkronos, 1 November 2016, www.adnkronos.com/morta-tina-anselmi-prima-donna-ministro_tylSeopuCpR7r8YBU1IuS?refresh_ce

Nardacci, Rossana, 'Tina Anselmi: Italy's first female minister', Italiani, 16 November 2016, www.italiani.it/en/tina-anselmi-the-Italian-woman-minister

'Obituary: Tina Anselmi', The Times, 5 November 2016, www.thetimes.co.uk/article/tina-anselmi-kvm3qhkqb

Olsen, Kirstin, Chronology of Women's History, Westport: Greenwood Press, 1994

Tambor, Molly, Lost Wave: Women and Democracy in Postwar Italy, New York: Oxford University Press US, 2014

'Tina Anselmi', enciclopediadelledonne.it, www.enciclopediadelledonne. it/biografie/tina-anselmi

'Tina Anselmi – ground-breaking politician', Italy on This Day, 25 March 2019, www.italyonthisday.com/2019/03/tina-anselmi-ground-breaking-politician.html

Wernham, Samantha, 'Obituary: Tina Anselmi, first female minister', The Italian Insider, 2 November 2016, www.italianinsider.it/ ?q=node/4538

Zwingle, Erla, 'The Garden of the Forgotten Venetians: The Partisan (Part 2: The Women)', I am not making this up, 20 January 2019, iamnotmakingthisup.net/tag/tina-anselmi

Vaira Vīķe-Freiberga

LATVIA

*In 1999 Vaira Vīķe-Freiberga was the
first woman to serve as president of Latvia*

'My parents never let me forget that I am Latvian,' said Vaira,
reflecting on her childhood, which was spent estranged from her
country. She was born in Riga in 1937 at the pivotal moment when
the Second World War was looming. Her father died at sea not
long after her birth and her mother remarried. In 1940 Latvia was
invaded and occupied by the Soviet Union, then by Nazi Germany,
and as the Soviet Union advanced to retake the country in 1944,
Vaira and her family fled. They made a perilous journey to Germany,
and she recalled, 'I still have certain nightmares that come from
that.' They found their way to Lübeck refugee camp in the north,
where conditions were very poor. Within three weeks of arriving,
her ten-month-old sister Mara contracted pneumonia and died,
while Vaira survived dysentery.

After the war Vaira's stepfather found work building a dam in
Morocco, where she attended a French school and learned French.
After five years the family moved to Canada, another country with
a new language to learn. Vaira was sixteen by this time, and rather
than finishing school, she got a job in a bank to help repay debts
the family owed as a result of their efforts to flee communism.
Vaira was determined not to lose her education and initially went
to evening classes and took courses by correspondence. By 1965
she had both a bachelor's and a master's degree and a PhD in
psychology. She became professor of psychology at the University

of Montreal, where she spent thirty-three years, becoming fluent in five languages.

Retiring from university life in 1998, Vaira took an unexpected phone call from the prime minister of Latvia. Latvia had declared independence in 1991 and by the mid-1990s Russian troops had withdrawn. Vaira was asked to become director of the newly founded Latvian Institute, which promoted Latvian culture internationally. After fifty-four years of exile, she returned to live in her homeland in June 1998. She came to public attention on the radio, speaking about her support for Latvian to become the country's official language, which made her a popular suggestion as a future president.

In the re-established Latvian Saeima (parliament), parties were jostling for position, and there was deadlock as none of the presidential candidates were able to obtain a majority. MPs from three parties recommended Vaira as a compromise candidate. She gave up her Canadian passport in order to run for election and won after seven rounds of voting with a majority of fifty-three to 100. Many Latvians had never heard of her and were shocked to find a woman with no political experience in the role, but her position as an independent and without the baggage of the previous party system was one of the reasons she enjoyed strong popularity.

Latvia had a troubled economy, and there were long-running tensions between the Latvian and Russian populations. Vaira was celebrated for being a plain-speaking president but also as a conciliatory figure who could work with politicians from any party. She won a second presidential term by a large majority and was a key player in securing membership of both NATO and the European Union for Latvia. She stepped down in 2007, a few months before her seventieth birthday, but has remained active on the international stage, serving as president of Club de Madrid, the world's largest forum of former heads of state and government, from 2014 to 2020.

'Curriculum vitae (until 1999)', Chancery of the President of Latvia, web.archive.org/web/20070927203356/www.president.lv/pk/content?cat_id=1891

'From child refugee to president: Latvia's Vaira Vike-Freiberga', BBC, 4 August 2019, www.bbc.co.uk/news/world-europe-49119077

Skard, Torild, *Women of Power: Half a Century of Female Presidents and Prime Ministers Worldwide*, Bristol: Policy Press, 2014

Stewart, Ashleigh, 'Former Latvian president and Montreal professor on Putin: "He's a narcissist and a psychopath"', Global News, 11 March 2022, globalnews.ca/news/8673073/vaira-vike-freiberga-latvia-ukraine-putin

'Vaira Vike-Freiberga', Britannica, www.britannica.com/biography/Vaira-Vike-Freiberga

Sylvie Kinigi

BURUNDI

In 1993 Sylvie Kinigi was the first woman
to serve as a prime minister in Africa

Sylvie Ntigashira struck lucky as a child because she was able to go
to school, something her eldest sister was denied as she had to help
in the home. Born in 1953 in Bujumbura, a rural province in what
was then Ruanda-Urundi, a colonial territory of Belgium, she was
the third of six children from a Tutsi family. She was taught at a
Belgian school by nuns and progressed to study economics at the
University of Burundi. In 1973 she married a Burundian academic,
Firmin Kinigi, who was ethnically Hutu. He supported Sylvie's
career, and the family hired a maid to take care of their house and
five children. After graduating she worked in Burundi's central
bank and taught at the university.

Sylvie became active in the women's organisation of the gov-
erning Tutsi party, the National Party for Unity and Progress
(UPRONA). A political moderate, she nonetheless pushed for
reform, becoming influential on economic and social measures for
women. She rose to be the organisation's head and a member of the
national executive board. In 1991 she became a special advisor to
the prime minister, responsible for carrying out economic reforms.

Urundi had become Burundi when it gained independence in
1962, but the following years had seen brutal civil war and conflict
resulting in hundreds of thousands of deaths. A window of hope
had opened when Burundi was able to mount its first democratic
elections in 1993, which were won by opposition leader Melchior

Ndadaye, a member of the Hutu ethnic majority. To promote unity, President Ndadaye created a cabinet of both Hutus and Tutsis and asked Sylvie to be prime minister. She reportedly was surprised and took time to accept the offer, eventually coming to the conclusion that she was no less qualified than the army officers who had been ruling the country. Hardliners from her own party were angered that she accepted the position.

After just three months in office the president was killed by insurgent Tutsi troops in an attempted coup. Ethnic violence broke out and Sylvie and members of the government took refuge in the French embassy. After a few days, Sylvie managed to gather together a majority of ministers to continue to govern, effectively becoming the acting president. She was able to hold the government together and create enough stability to allow the National Assembly to elect a new president in 1994, with Sylvie herself demonstrating a democratic transition by immediately stepping down. Creating enough stability to allow for a new government to take power was no small feat, Sylvie said. 'I wanted peace and normal conditions but my collaborators wanted me to declare a coup d'état. You can't carry on like that. When I managed to get a successor elected in a reasonably acceptable manner, I resigned.' However, the decline of state authority was too great, with the military eventually taking control, plunging Burundi into a war that wouldn't end until 2005.

· Sylvie went on to work at the United Nations among other international roles. She later returned to Burundi to work in economic development, where she advocated for the right of women to inherit land and property.

Appiah, Kwame Anthony and Gates Jr., Henry Louis (eds.), *Encyclopedia of Africa*, Oxford: Oxford University Press, 2010, p. 8

'Kinigi, Sylvie (1953–)', Encyclopedia.com, www.encyclopedia.com/women/dictionaries-thesauruses-pictures-and-press-releases/kinigi-sylvie-1953

Oluoch, Derrick, '12 little-known facts about Sylvia Kinigi, the first female President in Africa', The Standard, 19 March 2021,

www.standardmedia.co.ke/evewoman/amp/achieving-woman/
article/2001406840/12-little-known-facts-about-sylvie-kinigi-the-
first-female-president-in-africa

Skard, Torild, *Women of Power: Half a Century of Female Presidents and Prime Ministers Worldwide*, Bristol: Policy Press, 2014

'Sylvie Kinigi', Alchetron, alchetron.com/Sylvie-Kinigi

'Sylvie Kinigi', Britannica, www.britannica.com/biography/Sylvie-Kinigi

Miina Sillanpää

FINLAND

In 1907 Miina Sillanpää was one of the first nineteen women elected to the Finnish parliament, and in 1926 she was the first woman to serve as a minister

Finland was entering a terrible famine known as 'the great hunger years' when Vilhelmiina Riktig was born to poor peasant farmers in Jokioinen in 1866. Crop failure and unexpected weather had resulted in what would be Western Europe's last severe famine. Of Finland's population of 2 million, about 170,000 died of starvation. This brutal period made up her early years and she said that her childhood was so grey that there was nothing to tell about it.

Like other children from poor families, she attended a few classes at the 'visiting' school (a travelling teacher who moved between villages) while also working on the family croft and caring for younger siblings. She was only twelve when she started working twelve-hour shifts at a cotton mill for low wages and sleeping there in a dormitory. There were some lessons provided and Miina had a thirst for knowledge, appreciating the small education the mill provided, but she was largely self-taught. Later she would say that experience, rather than book learning, was her teacher.

Aged eighteen she chose her own name, Miina Sillanpää, and began working as a maid, later moving to the capital Helsinki to work as a domestic helper with various families for twelve years. Interested in the labour movement, she was elected to the committee which founded the Maids' Association and then elected as vice president. Embracing this new movement, she went to work for the Servants' Association and became the organisation's chair, dedicated to improving the rights and conditions of domestic workers, a position she held for the rest of her life.

A national general strike in 1905 created the environment for Miina to move closer to the political stage. Critics ridiculed her stance on servants' rights, calling her a home destroyer, but their attacks only made her more visible and popular as a key figurehead of the workers' movement and as a social democrat.

The unrest led to the establishment of universal suffrage, which included Finnish women, who were the first in Europe to win the right to vote in 1907. Miina was voted to the first parliament as one of the first of nineteen women MPs in Finland. She focused her work on children, families, elderly people and domestic servants. She fought for children who were born outside of marriage, and their mothers, creating a home association where they could live.

She was made minister for social affairs in 1926 and understood how exceptional her position was, saying, 'This has attracted attention everywhere. Many delegations have visited. Women especially want to greet me.' She worked to improve municipal homes, orphanages and care facilities for the poor and drafted laws for declaring women legally equal to men in marriage.

Miina was a member of the Finnish parliament for a total of thirty-eight years. Alongside her political career she worked as a journalist and for numerous associations and civic causes. She died in 1952 and the Miina Sillanpää Foundation was founded in 1965 to support elderly people. In 2016 the Finnish government made 1 October an official day in her honour. The Federation of Mother and Child Homes and Shelters, which Miina founded in 1945, still operates today, supporting women escaping domestic abuse.

Blanc, Eric, 'Finland's forgotten revolution', Links International Journal of Socialist Renewal, 4 June 2017, links.org.au/finland-forgotten-revolution-russian-empire-tsarism-independence-general-strike

Buchert, Peter, '150 years since the famine: The frost and fiscal policy brought the Finnish people to their knees', HBL, 7 October 2017, www.hbl.fi/artikel/150-ar-sedan-hungersnoden-frosten-och-finanspolitiken-fick-finska-folket-pa-kna

'Me as a Member of Parliament', Miina Sillanpään Seura, miinasillanpaaseura-fi.translate.goog/vaikuttaja/?_x_tr_sl= fi&_x_tr_tl=en&_x_tr_hl=en&_x_tr_pto=sc

'Miina Sillanpää', Academic, en-academic.com/dic.nsf/enwiki/2542024

'Miina Sillanpää Foundation', Miina Sillanpään Säätiö, www.miinasillanpaa.fi/eng

Miina Sillanpään Seura, 'Miina Sillanpää (with English subtitles)', YouTube, 8 April 2016, www.youtube.com/watch?v=jQwosjKbhH0

'Sillanpää, Miina (1866–1952)', Henkilöhistoria, kansallisbiografia.fi/kansallisbiografia/henkilo/788

'When everyone got the vote', This is Finland, finland.fi/life-society/when-everyone-got-the-vote

'Who is Miina Sillanpää?', Miina Sillanpään Seura, 2016, miinasillanpaaseura.fi/wp-content/uploads/2016/03/Miina-Sillanpaa-esite-eng.pdf

Joyce Banda

MALAWI

In 2012 Joyce Banda was the first
woman to serve as president of Malawi

Joyce Banda said she didn't have the chance to play like other children but that was how she learned leadership. Born in 1950 in Malemia, Nyasaland (now Malawi), she was the eldest of five children and helped to care for her siblings while her parents worked. Her family was able to send her to secondary school, but her best friend wasn't able to continue because of the fee. Joyce says this motivated her to devote her life to help girls go to school.

Joyce married Roy Kachale when she was twenty-one and had three children by the time she was twenty-five. He was appointed as a diplomat to Kenya and Joyce said that in Nairobi the work of the United Nations on women's rights woke her up to her own situation. She describes the marriage as blighted by domestic violence and alcohol abuse. The cultural pressure to remain married was high but she divorced, becoming destitute as a result and returning to Malawi, where she started a business to support her family. In 1983 she married Richard Banda, a barrister with four children. They had a further two children and adopted one, making a house of ten children which Joyce described as 'a mad house, but a happy one'.

She founded and directed various businesses, and while on a trip to the USA she came into contact with women's organisations. She was inspired to start a development commission back in Malawi and formed the National Association of Business Women, which saw her travelling the country and becoming a popular champion of gender equality. In 1997 she established the Joyce Banda Foundation to advance education and rural development for women and girls.

Having worked for many years for change, Joyce says she was frustrated with a lack of progress in improving lives through government. She ran for election in 1999 and won a parliamentary seat with the former ruling United Democratic Front party. In 2009 she ran alongside President Bingu wa Mutharika and won election as vice president, the first woman in Malawi to do so. However, Mutharike expelled her from the party following a dispute about succession. She weathered many efforts to remove her, including an assassination attempt, but continued to serve as vice president and founded the new People's Party.

In 2012 President Mutharika died in office. A brief period of constitutional uncertainty followed, but Joyce was sworn in as president and called for national unity. Her first move was to improve Malawi's international relations. As foreign donors returned, the country's economic growth rate more than doubled within two years, but Malawi's people remained largely in poverty. Joyce devalued the Malawian kwacha in an attempt to attract more donor funding, which prompted panic-buying. She introduced unpopular austerity measures, sold off a $15 million presidential jet and cut her own salary by 30 per cent.

In 2013, following issues over a corruption investigation, Joyce dissolved her entire cabinet. She cited this as a good example of her attempts to tackle corruption, but in 2014 she lost the election and failed to have it annulled.

Joyce continues to advocate for women's leadership internationally, saying, 'Africa has done more than any other continent, in terms of women in leadership... Tell me, how many women presidents America has had?'

Gillard, Julia and Okonjo-Iweala, Ngozi, *Women and Leadership: Real Lives, Real Lessons*, Australia: Vintage Books, 2020

House of Commons International Development Committee, *The Development Situation in Malawi: Volume II*, House of Commons, 24 July 2012, publications.parliament.uk/pa/cm201213/cmselect/cmintdev/118/118vw.pdf

'The Joyce Banda Foundation International', Facebook, www.facebook.com/The-Joyce-Banda-Foundation-International-410622789103893

'Joyce Banda: Malawi's first female president', BBC, 10 April 2012, www.bbc.co.uk/news/world-africa-17662916

Khunga, Suzgo, 'EW's big interview: Joyce Banda', The Nation, 21 September 2014, www.mwnation.com/ew%E2%80%99s-big-interview-joyce-banda

Mwagiru, Ciugu, 'Malawi's Joyce Banda and the rise of women in African politics', Daily Monitor, 18 April 2012, web.archive.org/web/20140606205525/www.monitor.co.ug/artsculture/Reviews/-/691232/1388740/-/diw45/-

National Association of Business Women, nabwmalawi.wixsite.com/website

Wahman, Michael, 'INTERVIEW: Joyce Banda and the inspirational effect of a female president', DIA, 20 April 2021, democracyinafrica.org/interview-joyce-banda-and-the-inspirational-effect-of-a-female-president

Berta Pīpiņa

LATVIA

In 1931 Berta Pīpiņa was the first
woman elected to the Latvian Saeima

Berta Pīpiņa once told an interviewer that her motivation to get elected was the smile on her husband's face when she voiced her opinions, saying, 'I swore that I would one day speak so well that no one would ever laugh at me.' Berta was born in 1883 in the parish of Code in the Russian Empire, now in Latvia. After attending school she moved into teaching, working in Kharkiv (now in Ukraine), and studied speech therapy for disabled children in Berlin. She travelled to Switzerland and Russia to widen her knowledge of educational techniques and in 1910 returned to Latvia and married Ermanis Pīpiņš, a journalist and literary critic, and had three children.

When Latvia broke away from the German Empire and declared independence in 1918, Berta became actively involved in politics. She co-founded the Democratic Centre Party and became the first woman elected to its central committee. In 1919 she was elected to Riga city council and went on to work on issues around destitution, public drinking and women and the family. She lectured on these subjects and wrote for newspapers and magazines.

Having participated in the work of the Latvian Women's National League for some time, in 1925 she was elected its president. She went on to be a co-founder and then leader of the Council of Latvian Women's Organisations, with one of its aims being to increase women's social and political influence. Five women had won seats in the Constitutional Assembly after independence, the first elected legislative body, but they made few political gains. After a constitution was agreed, the Saeima (parliament) was established. In 1931 Berta was elected to the fourth Saeima as a parliamentary deputy. She was the only woman elected and frequently drew attention to the effect of legislation on women and families. She argued for state support for mothers and families in the face of poverty, and notably disrupted a bill that required married women to give up paid employment. She was derided by prominent male politicians and in the press for her opinions.

In 1934 Berta set up the periodical *Latviete* (Latvian Woman), which called for equal rights for women and men and urged Latvian women to return to their rural roots, free from the foreign occupation of recent centuries. In that year Prime Minister Kārlis Ulmanis performed a coup, bringing in his own authoritarian regime and suspending the constitution. Berta withdrew from politics, turning her attention to her journalism and publishing a novel. When the Soviets occupied Latvia in 1940, she was considered an enemy of the state and in 1941 was deported to Siberia.

Berta died in a gulag, a forced labour camp used for political repression, on the Ob River in 1942. More than 1.5 million people are thought to have died in the Soviet camps between 1930 and 1953. During the Soviet period her biography was purged from encyclopaedias. Recognition of her important role as a pioneer only re-emerged after Latvia regained its independence in 1991.

'Berta Pīpiņa', Time Note, timenote.info/lv/Berta-Pipina

'Berta Pīpiņa (1883–1942?)', Bauskas Centrālā Bibliotēka,
    www.bauskasbiblioteka.lv/novadnieki-jubilari/items/363.html

De Haan, Francisca, Daskalova, Krassimira and Loutfi, Anna, *Biographical Dictionary of Women's Movements and Feminisms: Central, Eastern, and South Eastern Europe, 19th and 20th centuries*, Budapest: Central European University Press, 2006, pp. 432–5

Passmore, Kevin, *Women, Gender, and Fascism in Europe, 1919–45*, Manchester: Manchester University Press, 2003

Portia Simpson-Miller

JAMAICA

In 2006 Portia Simpson-Miller was the first
woman to serve as prime minister of Jamaica

Portia Lucretia Simpson was named by her father after the main female character in Shakespeare's *The Merchant of Venice*. She said of her father, 'He wanted me to be a lawyer. But I ended up being more than a lawyer because I became the first female prime minister of Jamaica. And I believe his spirit must have been celebrating that night when it was announced.' She was born into a poor rural family in Wood Hall, Jamaica, in 1945. They were politically active, supporting the People's National Party (PNP) and holding meetings in their house. Portia says her father was not an educated man but impressed on her the value of learning.

In 1974 she was asked to stand in the local elections and described it as a key moment in her life when she won. Local people saw her as one of them, and she said, 'I gained a lot of support because I had my hair natural... they were saying, "she could have been my daughter or granddaughter." They would hold my hand and take me to the other persons in the area and say, "you see this girl, we must give her our support."' Portia went on to win a seat in the House of Representatives for the PNP for the first time in 1976.

She became fondly referred to as Sista P but was also described in disparaging terms by her critics because of her Creole dialect and perceived lack of education. She says the criticism cut her despite the toughness she had built up as a politician. Nonetheless she thrived in parliament, first becoming the vice president of her party and leading its women's wing, and then in successive ministerial roles from 1989 onwards. Perhaps to defy her critics she also studied for a bachelor's degree in public administration, which she was awarded in 1997. The following year Portia married businessman Errald Miller and went on to have four children with him, adding his surname after hers.

In 2002 the PNP leader, Prime Minister P. J. Patterson, announced his intention to retire, and Portia won the leadership election against her two male rivals. She became prime minister of Jamaica in 2006 at age sixty, asking the people of Jamaica to be partners with her to promote human rights, create jobs and strengthen education. Crime went down and the economy grew, but she was damaged by a financial scandal in her administration and criticised for not providing speedy relief following Hurricane Dean in 2007. Portia's PNP narrowly lost the elections the following year and she went into opposition. She was elected as prime minister again in 2012. She reformed the country's drug laws and served for four years before stepping down in 2016.

Portia felt her experience was one that should be an inspiration to women from all backgrounds, saying, 'My journey is of the girl from Wood Hall that ended up in Jamaica House as prime minister, and it is not only a journey for me but a journey for all the girls, children and women of this country, who will now know that they, too, can achieve what they want to achieve in life.'

'First female prime minister: Portia Simpson Miller rewrote history', *The Gleaner*, go-jamaica.com/ja55/article.php?id=6

Jamaica Gleaner, 'Video: Portia talks politics, people, education and her rise to Prime Minister', YouTube, 8 March 2017, www.youtube.com/watch?v=Pbr9Rk1QC14

'Portia Simpson Miller', Britannica, www.britannica.com/biography/Portia-Simpson-Miller

Skard, Torild, *Women of Power: Half a Century of Female Presidents and Prime Ministers Worldwide*, Bristol: Policy Press, 2014

Virtue, Erica, 'Portia's pain – "It hurt most when they said I couldn't read"', *Jamaica Gleaner*, 19 January 2016, jamaica-gleaner.com/article/lead-stories/20160131/portias-pain-it-hurt-most-when-they-said-i-couldnt-read

Graça Machel

*In 1975 Graça Machel was the first woman
to serve as a cabinet minister in Mozambique*

Graça Machel's mother ensured all her children would be educated despite the family's difficult circumstances. Graça recalled, 'We didn't have much but we have never been poor. My mother gave us a very strong sense of dignity.' Consequently Graça attended a Methodist mission school from age six, which was highly unusual when over 90 per cent of women in Mozambique couldn't read or write in Portuguese. The youngest of six children, she was born in Gaza province in 1945 when Mozambique, known as Portuguese East Africa, was under Portuguese rule. Her father, a Methodist minister, had died in the weeks before her birth. With her mother's backing, Graça was one of a tiny minority of Black students at secondary school and continued to break through barriers by going to the University of Lisbon in Portugal on a scholarship, majoring in languages.

At university Graça became involved in the campaign for the liberation of Mozambique and was put under surveillance by the secret police, causing her to flee to Switzerland to avoid arrest. This paved her way to becoming a freedom fighter, joining Frelimo, the well-organised anti-colonial resistance movement. She went to Tanzania, where she received military training and started to teach children in organised schools. In this period she met Samora Machel, the head of Frelimo, who would become her husband and the future president.

The overthrow of the fascist government in Portugal was the catalyst for Mozambique to gain independence in 1975. Frelimo formed the interim government, and Graça was the country's first minister of education and the only woman in the cabinet at the age of twenty-nine. Under Graça, primary school enrolment went from 40 per cent to more than 90 per cent of boys and 75 per cent of girls, and literacy programmes for adults were introduced. However, the nation struggled to remain stable as it suffered under a brutal war waged by anti-Frelimo guerrillas funded by then-apartheid South Africa. In 1986 Graça's husband was killed in a suspicious plane crash that many blamed on South African interference.

Graça began working on projects related to the war's impact on children. The United Nations appointed her as an independent expert and her groundbreaking report recommended the rehabilitation of children affected by conflict. In 1995 Graça was awarded the Nansen Medal from the UN in recognition of her contribution to the welfare of refugee children, and she was successful in encouraging African governments to sign an international treaty banning the use of landmines.

Graça added First Lady to her numerous roles when she married president of South Africa Nelson Mandela in 1998. They had got to know each other when he became godfather to her children after the role was passed to him when African National Congress head Oliver Tambo died. Alongside her husband, Graça was a founding member of The Elders, an independent group of global leaders working for peace, justice and human rights.

Just as her mother had given her education as a child, Graça's legacy has been lifting up children. She said, 'Let us give a face and a voice to that girl child who has been ignored. When at last she is front and centre of our development efforts, it is she who will change the world.'

Arimus Media, 'ALD interview with Graca Machel', YouTube, 10 April 2015, www.youtube.com/watch?v=Hu7aK93qSME

'Dignity of Women biography: Graça Machel', Nelson Mandela Foundation, www.nelsonmandela.org/content/page/dignity-of-women-biography-gra%C3%A7a-machel

'Graça Machel', Beyond the Single Story, beyondthesinglestory.wordpress.com/2019/03/30/graca-machel

'Graça Machel', Britannica Kids, kids.britannica.com/kids/article/Gra%C3%A7a-Machel/602116

'Graça Machel', Learning for Justice, www.learningforjustice.org/classroom-resources/texts/graca-machel

'Graca Machel (1946–)', Women Leaders and Transformation in Developing Countries, people.brandeis.edu/~dwilliam/profiles/machel.htm

'Graça Simbine Machel', South African History Online, www.sahistory.org.za/people/graca-simbine-machel

'Machel, Graca Simbine 1945–', Encyclopedia.com, www.encyclopedia.com/education/news-wires-white-papers-and-books/machel-graca-simbine-1945

Saner, Emine, 'Graca Machel', *Guardian*, 8 March 2011, www.theguardian.com/world/2011/mar/08/graca-machel-100-women

Sheldon, Kathleen, 'An African leader: Graça Machel fights for women and children', UCLA Center for the Study of Women, 19 February 2021, csw.ucla.edu/2021/02/10/an-african-leader-graca-machel-fights-for-women-and-children

Leyla Zana

TURKEY

In 1991 Leyla Zana was the first Kurdish
woman elected to the Turkish parliament

'Today, women in Turkey rush to the streets and make their voices heard... In the past, they were shouting to exist as human beings... The view was: If you are a man, you have value; if you are a woman, you don't. This narrow-mindedness had to be shattered,' said Leyla Zana.

Leyla was born in 1961 in the south-east of Turkey to a Kurdish family. Kurds are the largest ethnic minority in Turkey and have faced longstanding state repression, including bans on their language. Though Leyla wanted to remain at school, her father allowed her only eighteen months of education, leaving her illiterate. She says she never conformed: 'At nine years old I attacked my forty-five-year-old uncle for beating my aunt. I have always been a combatant.'

At fourteen she was married to a cousin twenty years her senior, Mehdi Zana. Leyla says although she was distressed, she had grown up having no say in her life, and this was no different. Later in her career she would speak against child marriage. Mehdi was active in the Turkish communist workers' party and became mayor of Diyarbakır. A military coup in 1980 led to his imprisonment for the next ten years.

Leyla was now a young single mother of one child and pregnant with a second. She has said she didn't know how she would survive. But she learned to read and write alongside her children, slowly finding her voice, and by 1984 was taking part in political activities. She worked in the local human rights association and became a popular organiser. In 1988 Leyla was arrested, accused of inciting people to revolt. Like other political prisoners, she says she was stripped naked and subjected to electric torture. More determined than ever, she won a seat in parliament in 1991, receiving 84 per cent of her district's vote for the Social Democratic Party.

In her most famous act, Leyla took the parliamentary oath in Turkish, then added a Kurdish sentence, while wearing a headband of yellow, red and green – the Kurdish colours. The Kurdish language had been recently legalised to be spoken in private, but was still illegal in public. The footage shows parliamentarians shouting in outrage as they bang desks. Her final line in Kurdish caused uproar: 'I take this oath for the brotherhood between the Turkish people and the Kurdish people.'

Accused of being a separatist and a terrorist, Leyla was protected from prosecution as an MP. In 1993 she joined the new Kurdish Democracy Party, but in 1994 the party was banned and Leyla was charged with treason and accused of connections to the militant Kurdistan Workers' Party (PKK), which she vehemently denied. Leyla spent ten years in prison, and was recognised as a 'prisoner of conscience' by Amnesty International and nominated for the Nobel Peace Prize. In 1995 the European Parliament awarded her the Sakharov Prize for Freedom of Thought, in recognition of her work for human rights. As international pressure increased, in 2004 the High Court of Appeals ordered her release from prison.

Leyla returned to activism and was re-elected to parliament. She made headlines in 2012, when she met Prime Minister Erdoğan to discuss the Kurdish–Turkish peace process, something that seemed unthinkable previously. However, Leyla continued to face persecution, most recently in 2018 having her parliamentary membership revoked. She continues to work for peace.

HRH in Bergen, 'Leyla Zana sentenced to prison', Human Rights House, 31 July 2009, humanrightshouse.org/articles/leyla-zana-sentenced-to-prison

'Leyla Zana', The Kurdish Project, thekurdishproject.org/history-and-culture/famous-kurds-old/leyla-zana

'Leyla Zana – 1995, Turkey', Sakharov Prize European Parliament, www.europarl.europa.eu/sakharovprize/en/leyla-zana-1995-turkey/products-details/20200330CAN54170

'Leyla Zana biography', Peace in Kurdistan, www.peaceinkurdistan campaign.com/resources/leyla-zana/leyla-zana-biography

'Leyla Zana: European Parliament's Sakharov Prize Winner of 1995', European Parliament, www.europarl.europa.eu/meetdocs/2004_2009/documents/fd/nt_zana_/nt_zana_en.pdf

Sert, Aysegul, 'A woman, a Kurd, and an optimist', *New York Times*, 19 February 2013, www.nytimes.com/2013/02/20/world/europe/20iht-letter20.html

'Turkey gives Kurdish MP Leyla Zana 10-year sentence', BBC, 24 May 2012, www.bbc.co.uk/news/world-us-canada-18188426

Maureen Colquhoun

UNITED KINGDOM

In 1976 Maureen Colquhoun was the UK's
first out LGBT+ member of parliament

In her later years, Maureen Colquhoun's reputation has been revived by those seeing her as a trailblazer for LGBT+ politicians. During her time in politics, however, she suffered career-ending prejudice and in 2017 received an apology letter for her treatment from her former constituency. Born in 1928 in Eastbourne in southern England, Maureen was brought up by her Irish mother, a single parent. Interested in politics from a young age, she joined the Labour Party at seventeen, studied economics, and at age twenty married Keith Colquhoun, a journalist. They went on to have three children.

Maureen spent time raising her family but stepped back into politics when her children were older, and was elected to Shoreham council in 1965. She wanted to stand for parliament next, but like many women she was unlikely to be placed in a safe seat and lost in her first attempt in 1970. In a candid interview ahead of the 1974 general election when she was forty-five years old, she said, 'If you don't make up your mind, round about your twenties, that you're going in for a political career, you tend to get trapped by a man, and Keith Colquhoun trapped me.' Despite the marginal status of the seat under contention, Northampton North, Maureen won and threw herself into her new life in Westminster.

Maureen was a forward-thinking feminist and campaigned to abolish women's prisons, decriminalise prostitution and relax abortion law. While working on the 1975 Sex Discrimination Act she met Barbara Todd, co-editor of the lesbian magazine *Sappho*. They next worked together on a bill to create equal representation in public bodies and were drawn to each other. Maureen explained, 'By the time the House met to debate the second reading of the Balance of the Sexes Bill, I knew that Babs loved me and she knew that I loved her.'

Maureen quickly came out to her family, was publicly open about her relationship and moved to London with her new partner. No announcement was made, but she asked the speaker of the House of Commons to alter her title from Mrs to Ms or to give her no title. A gossip column in the *Daily Mail* newspaper broke the story about her relationship and her family became the focus of pursuit by tabloid journalists. Her party was alarmed at her regular outings in the press on this subject and others, such as when she brought fifty sex workers to a parliamentary committee room for the first reading of her Protection of Prostitutes bill.

When it came to the next election, Maureen found herself without political allies and her local party chairman was reported as saying, 'She was elected as a working wife and mother... this business has blackened her image irredeemably.' She wasn't selected again for the seat, and it is widely thought that prejudice about her sexuality was the cause. She appealed against the move and won, but still lost her seat to the Conservative candidate in the 1979 election.

Maureen never made it back to parliament. She worked for Gingerbread, the charity for single-parent families, and also for the Labour Party, and served as a councillor in the Hackney borough of London for eight years. After same-sex marriage was legalised in the UK, Maureen and Barbara married. When Maureen died in 2021, she was buried with Barbara with a gravestone reading 'They loved one another'.

Campbell, Lucy, 'Maureen Colquhoun, the UK's first openly lesbian MP, dies aged 92', *Guardian*, 2 February 2021, www.theguardian.com/

politics/2021/feb/02/maureen-colquhoun-the-uks-first-openly-lesbian-mp-dies-aged-92?fbclid=IwAR2W0vW6J89-hv8LLRhgb QLkRLKEu4XTpcQDSiEn8CFJpxj8jDZcpG5qI2g

Chant, Holly, 'Maureen Colquhoun remembered as "political fighter for justice and truth"', *Hackney Gazette*, 1 March 2021, www.hackneygazette.co.uk/news/obituaries/former-hackney-councillor-maureen-colquhoun-obituary-7794014

Colquhoun, Maureen, *A Woman in the House*, UK: Scan, 1980

Colquhoun, Maureen, Howlett, Ivan and Warbis, Chris, 'Maureen Colquhoun', BBC Radio Brighton, British Library Sound Archives, 5 September 1973

Langdon, Julia, 'Maureen Colquhoun obituary', *Guardian*, 8 February 2021, www.theguardian.com/politics/2021/feb/08/maureen-colquhoun-obituary

Lewis, Helen, *Difficult Women: A History of Feminism in 11 Fights*, London: Jonathan Cape, 2020

Marchant-Wallis, Caroline, 'Listening to Maureen Colquhoun', University of Sussex, 2 July 2021, blogs.sussex.ac.uk/librarycollections/2021/07/02/listening-to-maureen-colquhoun

Marsh, Megan and Armitage, Louise, 'Maureen Colquhoun – first openly gay woman in Parliament', LSE, 13 February 2019, blogs.lse.ac.uk/lsehistory/2019/02/13/maureen-colquhoun

Sturgess, Sammy, 'Maureen Colquhoun: "an open lesbian feminist woman" in the House of Commons', The History of Parliament, 18 February 2020, thehistoryofparliament.wordpress.com/2020/02/18/maureen-colquhoun-an-open-lesbian-feminist-woman-in-the-house-of-commons

Cristina Fernández de Kirchner

ARGENTINA

*In 2007 Cristina Fernández de Kirchner was the
first woman to be elected president of Argentina*

Women who lead Latin American countries, and of course particularly Argentina, are almost always compared to Eva Perón, but Evita never faced an election. Yet the name Perón continues to dominate Argentinian politics and Cristina Fernández de Kirchner is a Perónist – a loose term describing those who still follow former President Juan Perón's policies of social justice, economic nationalism and political sovereignty.

Cristina was born in 1953 in La Plata; her mother was a Perónist trade union leader while her father ran a bus company, giving her a comfortable childhood. She went to law school and met her husband Néstor Kirchner, and the couple got involved in the Perónist Party in the 1970s. In 1976 the military junta ousted unelected President Isabel Perón and the Kirchners fled to the south of the country and started a law firm.

In the 1980s Cristina and her husband were both elected to provincial parliament, and in 1991 Néstor was elected governor of Santa Cruz. She supported him as a deputy, a pattern of working that they would flip and repeat throughout their careers. Of the two of them, she made the leap to the national level first, getting elected to the Senate in 1995 and the Chamber of Deputies in 1997. She came to national prominence at this time for criticising the president, Carlos Menem, for illegal arms sales and corruption.

Néstor Kirchner was first in the marriage to take the presidency, winning in 2003. Cristina didn't join him on the podium, preferring to be known as 'First Citizen' rather than 'First Lady'. However, she worked with fervour to get his bills into law and was involved in almost every decision, having much more influence than an elected politician would otherwise.

Her husband served one term and then swung behind his wife to stand in the next presidential election. In the face of the macho Argentine culture, Cristina endured criticism less of her policies and more of her appearance, and accusations that she owed her position to her husband. She said that women 'always have to pass a double test: first, show that because we are women we are not idiots, and second, the one that anyone has to take'.

She won the 2007 presidential election with 45 per cent of the vote. In power, she promised to improve education and the public health system and to make Argentina a human rights model. When the global financial crisis struck in 2008, Cristina's government struggled to maintain stability, and lost its majority in both chambers.

In 2010 Néstor died suddenly, and Cristina turned to wearing black and emphasising her intention to maintain his memory through implementing his policies. In the 2012 elections she won with the largest margin since democratic elections had begun in 1983. In 2013 she was forced to take time off for bleeding in the brain. The two term limit prevented Cristina from standing at the 2015 presidential election, and her preferred candidate went on to lose against a background of repeated accusations of corruption related to her time in office. This didn't prevent her election as vice president in 2019 or mar her popularity with those most affected by the new government's austerity measures. A charge of 'treason', which was labelled as unsubstantiated by Human Rights Watch, was dismissed in 2021, as well as a charge of fraud.

'Argentina: far-fetched "treason" charges against ex-officials', Human Rights Watch, 19 December 2017, www.hrw.org/news/2017/12/19/argentina-far-fetched-treason-charges-against-ex-officials

'Argentine judge dismisses case against ex-President Fernandez',
  Reuters, 8 October 2021, www.reuters.com/world/americas/
  argentine-judge-says-there-was-no-crime-case-against-ex-president-
  fernandez-2021-10-08
'Cristina Fernández de Kirchner', Iowa State University Archives of
  Women's Political Communication, awpc.cattcenter.iastate.edu/
  directory/cristina-fernandez-de-kirchner
'Cristina Kirchner interview with *The New Yorker* – up close and uncut',
  Cristina Fernández de Kirchner, 11 March 2015, www.cfkargentina.
  com/interview-with-the-new-yorker
'"Dollar futures": Case against Cristina Fernández de Kirchner
  dismissed', *Buenos Aires Times*, 13 April 2021, www.batimes.com.ar/
  news/argentina/dolar-futures-judges-dismiss-case-against-cristina-
  fernandez-de-kirchner.phtml
Goñi, Uki, 'Cristina's comeback: Fernández de Kirchner set for
  dramatic return as Argentina's No 2', *Guardian*, 24 October 2019,
  www.theguardian.com/world/2019/oct/24/christina-de-fernandez-
  kirchner-argentina-marci
'Kirchner: The First Female President of a Machista Society', Center for
  Conflict Studies, sites.miis.edu/ccsprofilesofworldleaders/2013/12/
  22/kirchner-the-first-female-president-of-a-machista-society
'Profile: Cristina Fernández de Kirchner', BBC, 7 December 2022,
  www.bbc.co.uk/news/world-latin-america-12284208
Skard, Torild, *Women of Power: Half a Century of Female Presidents and Prime
  Ministers Worldwide*, Bristol: Policy Press, 2014

Ella Koblo Gulama

SIERRA LEONE

In 1957 Ella Koblo Gulama was the first woman elected to
the House of Representatives of Sierra Leone, and in 1963
she was the first woman cabinet minister in West Africa

Ella Gulama, born in 1921, grew up as the daughter of King Julius Gulama (re-named as Paramount Chief under British rule) of Kaiyamba Kingdom, one of the founders of the Sierra Leone People's Party, the party Ella would rise through. Though he had many children, she spent time with her father learning about the kingdom, the traditional political system and accompanying him as he decided on 'palavas', or disputes, between his people. She did well at school and attended a women's teacher-training college, highly unusual for a young woman and especially the daughter of a king. After completing her studies she was appointed supervising teacher for the Southern Province, the first woman to hold the position.

In 1946 Ella was arranged to be married to King Bai Kobolo Pathbanall of the Port Loko District, a marriage that her father saw as building a bridge between regions. Her new husband had many wives, like other kings, and Ella found it difficult to adapt to her situation, at one point secretly leaving and returning home. However, after discussions she returned and found a role for herself accompanying her husband to political meetings and conferences.

When Ella's father died in 1951, sixteen candidates contested his position, with Ella being the only woman. In the election among the tribal authorities Ella won over 60 per cent of the vote, but there had never been a female ruler in Kaiyamba Kingdom and her critics blocked her from the role. Ella took the matter to the British House of Commons, whose members agreed she should be elected. Nonetheless, she was forced to go through another round of voting. She won with 74 per cent of the vote two years after her father had died. Madam Ella, as she became known, was the first woman to be queen in Kaiyamba Kingdom.

In 1957 it was announced that elections would include seats for Paramount Chiefs to become members of the House of Representatives in Freetown, the capital of Sierra Leone, and Ella said she chose to stand 'to contribute to the nation-building and to show my people that women can take their places side by side with the men folk'. She won and was the only woman in the House for five years. Sierra Leone achieved independence in 1961 and the parliament became a fully elected body. Ella was re-elected and appointed a cabinet minister in the government of Sir Milton Margai, Sierra Leone's first prime minister.

When the prime minister died and his half-brother replaced him, Ella supported him and regained her seat in 1967. However, the elections were followed by instability affecting the whole country, resulting in a series of military coups that created a thirty-year period of rule under the All People's Congress, the opposition party. They suspended the constitution and dissolved parliament. Charged with treason, Ella spent two and a half years in prison and was deposed as queen. She spent time working for the United Methodist Church and became president of the National Organisation for Women. In 1992 the government was overthrown, and Ella was able to stand again for election as queen, winning a huge majority and breaking down in tears when she was handed the 'staff of office'. She died in 2006 in Kaiyamba Kingdom.

Jalloh, Abu Bakarr, 'Queen Ella Koblo Gulama: the first elected female member of parliament in Sierra Leone and the first female minister in Sub-Saharan Africa', The African Dream, 8 February 2022, theafricandreamsl.com/queen-ella-koblo-gulama-the-first-

elected-female-member-of-parliament-in-sierra-leone-and-the-first-
female-minister-in-sub-saharan-africa

'The life and times of Honourable PC Madam Ella Koblo Gulama of
Sierra Leone', Awareness Times, 26 September 2006, web.archive.org/
web/20080119070704/news.sl/drwebsite/publish/article_20053696.
shtml

Lucan, Talabi Aisie, *The Life and Times of Paramount Chief Madam Ella Koblo
Gulama MBE; OBE, MRSL*, Sierra Leone Association of Writers and
Illustrators, 2003

'Madam Ella Koblo Gulama is dead', The Patriotic Vanguard,
10 September 2006, www.thepatrioticvanguard.com/madam-ella-
koblo-gulama-is-dead

Birtukan Mideksa

ETHIOPIA

*In 2008 Birtukan Mideksa was the first woman
to lead a major political party in Ethiopia*

Birtukan Mideksa has said that although her family faced material challenges when she was a child, she received 'a good deal of love'. She was born in 1974 in a small village on the outskirts of the Ethiopian capital Addis Ababa, and her mother took care of the family; her father had been in the military, but was a pensioner when she was born. Birtukan was interested in justice from a young age but knew it was an unusual career choice for women. She recalled, 'There was a judge in the supreme court of the country. She was the only one on the bench when I watched some episode in a public television broadcast. I was excited to see her in that kind of position.'

After high school, she studied law at Addis Ababa University and applied to join the federal court, working as a clerk before being recruited as a judge in the First Instance Court. At twenty-six she ran for parliament and failed to get elected but saw it as a learning experience to understand the needs of the people in her community.

In 2002 Birtukan presided over the high-profile case of former defence minister Siye Abraha, who was accused of corruption after falling out with President Meles Zenawi. She released Abraha on bail but minutes later government authorities rearrested him as he walked out of court. In cases like this she was in direct conflict with the government in her attempt to maintain judicial independence, which eventually led her to resign.

In 2005 she was a founder of the opposition Coalition for Unity and Democracy (CUD). The group of parties was formed to present a united front against the ruling Ethiopian People's Revolutionary Democratic Front (EPRDF) in the 2005 election. Hopes were high that Ethiopia could move from largely single-party rule to a multi-party democracy. However, the CUD cited repression and vote rigging when the EPRDF claimed power and protesters took to the streets. In the resulting violence Ethiopian police massacred 193 protesters. Birtukan was among thousands of people who were detained, and she was accused of treason and jailed for life, leaving behind a daughter to be cared for by her elderly mother.

She was pardoned after eighteen months, and, her party having been banned, she set about creating a new coalition and was elected as its chair, despite her mother's pleas for her to go into exile. After discussing the circumstances of her pardon while on a trip to Europe, she was rearrested and spent another twenty-one months in detention, including two months in solitary confinement without visits from her daughter. There was international condemnation of her imprisonment, and she was freed again in 2010, going into exile in the USA. Speaking about the role of Ethiopian women in political opposition, Birtukan said, 'You find very strong women in every level who dare to defy, and who committed their life to pay the price necessary for this noble cause, but... we don't see the participation of women in political leadership and political participation as we need to.'

The election of reformer Abiy Ahmed as prime minister in 2018 paved the way for Birtukan to return home. He recommended her as chair of the National Election Board of Ethiopia to oversee the election in 2021. Ahmed said she was the right person for the job because she would 'never surrender, even to the government'. The elections passed peacefully, and while some cast doubt on their legitimacy, Birtukan said the board had delivered Ethiopia's first 'credible election'.

'2005 Ethiopian election: a look back', VOA, 16 May 2010, www.voanews.com/a/article-2005-ethiopian-election-a-look-back-93947294/159888.html

'Abiy Ahmed sworn in as Ethiopia's prime minister', Al Jazeera, 2 April 2018, www.aljazeera.com/news/2018/4/2/abiy-ahmed-sworn-in-as-ethiopias-prime-minister

'Birtukan Mideksa: Ethiopia's electoral board chairperson', BBC, 21 June 2021, www.bbc.co.uk/news/world-africa-57486959

'Ethiopian protesters "massacred"', BBC, 19 October 2006, news.bbc.co.uk/1/hi/world/africa/6064638.stm

'Interviews: Birtukan Mideksa', The Freedom Collection, www.freedomcollection.org/interviews/birtukan_midekssa/?vidid=729

Mideksa, Birtukan, 'Prisoners of conscience in Ethiopia', Al Jazeera, 30 March 2013, www.aljazeera.com/opinions/2013/3/30/prisoners-of-conscience-in-ethiopia

Rice, Xan, 'Jailed but not forgotten: Birtukan Mideksa, Ethiopia's most famous prisoner', Guardian, 9 January 2010, www.theguardian.com/world/2010/jan/09/jailed-birtukan-mideksa-ethiopia-prisoner

Tessema, Seleshi and Getachew, Addis, 'Profile – Birtukan Mideskksa: Ethiopia's symbol of electoral reform', AA, 19 June 2021, www.aa.com.tr/en/africa/profile-birtukan-mideksa-ethiopia-s-symbol-of-electoral-reform/2279521

Yared, Tegbaru, 'Ethiopia's election was peaceful but not competitive', Institute for Security Studies, 5 July 2021, issafrica.org/iss-today/ethiopias-election-was-peaceful-but-not-competitive

Jadranka Kosor

CROATIA

In 2009 Jadranka Kosor was the first
woman to serve as prime minister of Croatia

In her recent biography, the formerly private Jadranka Kosor revealed details about her childhood, including local dances and happy cycling trips with her mother, but she also described the legacy of male violence in her life. Born in Lipik in the west of Croatia in 1953, she says her parents started fighting as soon as she was born, and her mother, a teacher, often came to school in overalls because her father was jealous and violent and didn't allow her to wear a dress. Her parents divorced when she was two, and she lived with her grandmother while her mother worked away from home. She describes gaining skills and independence from her grandmother, doing her own laundry and cooking at the age of four. Jadranka relates how when her mother returned with a new husband, he physically abused her mother and tried to get into bed with Jadranka when she was fifteen. She says, 'I kicked him out,' and recalls having support from her grandmother, who had also suffered violence at the hands of her grandfather.

Despite the numerous challenges she faced, Jadranka excelled at high school. She enjoyed music and was a keen writer, publishing a book of poems titled *Koraci (Steps)* when she was eighteen. She studied law at the University of Zagreb and began working part-time at Radio Zagreb, and then as a journalist for *Večernji list*, a Croatian daily newspaper. When, in 1991, Croatia declared independence from Yugoslavia (a country made up of six socialist republics formed after the Second World War), the brutal wars that followed the country's break-up displaced hundreds of thousands of people, and Jadranka became well known for hosting a radio show for refugees and disabled veterans.

By then the transition from the one-party system was under way in Croatia. In 1989 Jadranka had joined the centre-right Croatian Democratic Union (HDZ) and risen quickly through the ranks. In 1990 the first Croatian multi-party elections were held and HDZ's Dr Franjo Tudjman was elected president. The new electoral system had seen a big reduction in the number of women in parliament, and Tudjman urged Jadranka to stand. In 1995 she was elected to parliament and also became party vice president. The HDZ created a Women's Association with Jadranka as its leader and she was credited with doubling the number of women standing in the 2000 elections.

In 2003 she became minister for family, veterans and intergenerational solidarity. When the prime minister unexpectedly resigned in 2009, he proposed Jadranka as his successor. She inherited a country with severe economic problems and a border conflict with Slovenia. She promised to create the conditions for recovery and for Croatia to become a member of the European Union. She took a strong stance against corruption and removed politicians suspected of being corrupt, including in her own party. In 2011 she signed the accession treaty in Brussels and her promise to take Croatia into the EU was kept.

Jadranka lost the 2011 elections and then lost leadership of her party, eventually being expelled from HDZ for claims of damaging the party's reputation. Jadranka received little support from her colleagues. Despite this, she has no regrets about her career, saying, 'I fell in love with that job, I was in a party for a long time, I met a lot of great people there, I really felt like "in the family".'

'Independent Croatia', Britannica, www.britannica.com/place/Croatia/ Independent-Croatia#ref1060949

'Jadranka Kosor', Council of Women World Leaders, www.councilwomenworldleaders.org/jadranka-kosor.html

'Jadranka Kosor', VL, 1 December 2016, www.vecernji.hr/enciklopedija/jadranka-kosor-18120

'Jadranka Kosor about childhood traumas', Slobodna Dalmacija, 12 July 2020, slobodnadalmacija.hr/vijesti/hrvatska/jadranka-kosor-o-traumama-iz-djetinjstva-otac-je-moju-majku-poceo-tuci-cim-sam-se-rodila-a-ocuh-mi-se-kad-sam-imala-15-godina-uvukao-u-krevet-1032030

'Kosor becomes first woman PM', France 24, 7 July 2009, www.france24.com/en/20090707-kosor-first-woman-prime-minister-croatia

Kosor, Jadranka, 'Former Croatian PM Jadranka Kosor talks current events, future plans', Total Croatia News, 17 February 2016, www.total-croatia-news.com/politics/2508-former-croatian-pm-jadranka-kosor-talks-current-events-future-plans

Turner, Barry (ed.), *The Statesman's Yearbook 2012: The Politics, Cultures and Economies of the World*, London: Palgrave Macmillan UK, 2017, p. 371

Isabel Ursula Teshea

TRINIDAD AND TOBAGO

*In 1961 Isabel Ursula Teshea was the first woman elected
to the Trinidad and Tobago House of Representatives,
and in 1963 she was the first woman minister*

Described as self-effacing and charming, Isabel Ursula Cadogan
was born in Princes Town in 1911 and displayed leadership qualities from a young age. She became a pupil-teacher after finishing
her own primary schooling. There was little access to secondary
education at the time and the pupil-teacher system allowed her
to act as an apprentice, giving her a first opportunity to pursue a
career at a time when women largely worked in the home. It was at
this young age that Isabel began her lifelong work in community
and social work, organising concerts, dances and debates, and supporting people in need through her local church.

She went on to clerical work on a sugar estate, eventually moving to Trinidad's capital, Port of Spain, to work in stock control at
a technology company. She married Roy Teshea in 1938, but the
marriage did not last, perhaps unsurprising in a social climate that
was intolerant of working women. She also pursued further education, enrolling at the University of Puerto Rico to study community
education.

Isabel was an early member of the People's National Movement
(PNM), the party that led the country to independence from over
150 years of British colonial rule. She organised many women's
groups and was a founding member and the chair of the PNM
Women's League. Isabel's talent for organisation and her network

of groups would form a key part in winning elections for the PNM because her women members canvassed door to door. She rose in prominence and became vice chair of the PNM in 1956, the first woman to hold the post.

As the country moved towards full independence, a House of Representatives and Senate were created, and elections were held in 1961. Isabel stood for the Port of Spain East District, winning by more than 7,000 votes. She became parliamentary secretary to the minister of local government and community development, rising to become minister of health and housing.

In 1970 Isabel was appointed ambassador to Ethiopia and from 1974 high commissioner to Guyana, a post she held until her retirement in 1977, when she quietly withdrew from public life. In 1981 she was the recipient of the Trinity Cross, the country's highest honour, for public service, an award made posthumously since she died earlier that year at the age of sixty-nine.

'Big victory', *Kingston Gleaner*, 6 December 1961, newspaperarchive.com/
  politics-clipping-dec-06-1961-429977

Geilen, Matthews, 'Teshea, Ursula Isabel', 2016, www.researchgate.net/
  publication/339214931_Teshea_Ursula_Isabel

Palmer, Colin A., *Encyclopedia of African-American Culture and History:
  The Black Experience in the Americas*, Macmillan Reference USA, 2006,
  p. 2182

'Teshea, Isabel', Encyclopedia.com, www.encyclopedia.com/history/
  encyclopedias-almanacs-transcripts-and-maps/teshea-isabel

'Williams shuffles cabinet', *Kingston Gleaner*, 18 May 1963,
  newspaperarchive.com/politics-clipping-may-18-1963-430003

Golda Meir

ISRAEL

*In 1969 Golda Meir was the first woman
to be elected prime minister of Israel*

Golda Meir described her early life as coloured by poverty and fear. Born Goldie Mabovitch in 1898, in Kyiv, Ukraine, she and her family were among the 2 million Jews who fled to escape pogroms (mob attacks) carried out in the Russian Empire, killing hundreds. Her childhood terror of antisemitic violence strongly influenced her life's work. The family emigrated to Milwaukee in the USA and in her teens Golda joined the Labor Zionist movement, which combined socialism with the international movement for the establishment of a Jewish national state. Her sister Shayna had risked her life in Ukraine to attend Labor Zionist meetings, and now Shayna's radical friends influenced Golda's developing political philosophy. Golda went on to qualify as a teacher despite the objections of her parents, who felt that girls should be married rather than pursue a profession.

Golda married Morris Myerson in 1917 (later modifying her name to Meir) on the condition that they would emigrate to Palestine and live on a kibbutz. They joined Kibbutz Merhavia, where residents shared everything and worked as a collective. While Golda thrived, her husband became ill and refused to have children unless it was in a conventional family setting. They moved to Jerusalem and had two children, while living in poverty. At this time Golda was offered a job as secretary of the Women Workers' Council at Histadrut (the General Federation of Workers). Knowing her husband would not approve, she moved with her children to Tel Aviv, signalling the end of her marriage. She later discussed worries over her children's upbringing but said, 'There is a type of woman who cannot let her husband and children narrow her horizons.'

Golda rose through the ranks of Histadrut, becoming part of its 'inner circle'. During the Second World War, she held key posts in the World Zionist Organization and the Jewish Agency, which functioned as the government, and in 1948 was a signatory of Israel's independence declaration. Arab states opposed the declaration, and as a result a few days later five Arab armies massed on the newly established borders. Meir disguised herself as a Muslim woman and crossed into Jordan for a secret meeting with King Abdullah in an unsuccessful attempt to avoid war.

She served as minister of labour, providing subsidised housing for immigrants and integrating them into the workforce while Palestinians were forced from their homes under her tenure. As minister of foreign affairs she initiated Israel's historically successful alliance with the USA.

After the death of Prime Minister Levi Eshkol in 1969, and despite poor health and a few years of retirement, Golda emerged as the 'consensus candidate' to stand as prime minister and she led a coalition to victory. Shortly after she took office, the War of Attrition (military conflict along the Suez Canal) ended in a ceasefire agreement and a period of peace. However, the Fourth Arab–Israeli War saw Golda's government condemned for its lack of preparedness, leading her to resign in 1974.

She died in 1978, and it was revealed that she had been suffering from cancer of the blood for twelve years. Her legacy is that of an uncompromising stateswoman who played a role in securing the future of the Israeli state. She remains one of the most visible women in international affairs in the twentieth century.

'Golda Meir', Britannica, www.britannica.com/biography/Golda-Meir

Pogrebin, Letty Cottin, 'Golda Meir', Jewish Women's Archive, jwa.org/encyclopedia/article/meir-golda

Silverstein, Jordana, 'How Golda Meir, Israel's "Iron Lady", helped establish an independent Jewish state', The Conversation, 17 July 2021, theconversation.com/how-golda-meir-israels-iron-lady-helped-establish-an-independent-jewish-state-156374

Soussi, Alasdair, 'The mixed legacy of Golda Meir, Israel's first female PM', Al Jazeera, 18 March 2019, www.aljazeera.com/features/2019/3/18/the-mixed-legacy-of-golda-meir-israels-first-female-pm

Jeannette Rankin

UNITED STATES OF AMERICA

In 1916 Jeannette Rankin was the first
woman elected to the US Congress

When Jeannette Rankin was elected, she was treated as a curiosity by the press rather than taken seriously. The *Journal Gazette* of Fort Wayne, Indiana, described her as 'a grey-eyed, slender girl with the enthusiasm of a zealot, the simplicity of a child and the energy and fire of a race horse'. Perhaps unlike the gentlemen of the press, Jeannette, who was born in 1880, had experience of seeing men and women working together as relative equals during her childhood: she learned to build, maintain machinery and do chores alongside everyone on her family's successful ranch near Missoula, Montana.

After graduating from high school, Jeannette studied biology at university when further education was still unusual for women. A visit to Boston, where she saw urban slums, led her to work in a settlement house for poor women and children and then to study social work. While on campus at the University of Washington, she joined the campaign for women's suffrage, becoming an organiser for the New York Woman Suffrage Party.

In 1911 Jeannette's political career started to emerge as she returned to Montana and became the first woman to argue for women's suffrage in front of the state legislature. For the next few years she travelled widely, leading the state campaign, and in 1914 the public voted in a referendum to give women in Montana the franchise. Naturally Jeannette declared her candidacy for one of the state's two seats in Congress in 1916, running as a Republican on the issues of universal suffrage, child welfare and opposition to the First World War. When Jeanette won, the majority of women still didn't have the right to vote. Like many first elected women, she felt the weight of her role as a pioneer, and commented, 'I am deeply conscious of the responsibility... I will not only represent the women of Montana, but also the women of the country, and I have plenty of work cut out for me.'

On her first day in the House she introduced a bill to guarantee women's suffrage in the US Constitution, which would later become the 19th Amendment. This would eventually pass in 1920; however, many women, but particularly women of colour, were still prevented from casting a ballot for many years to come.

On her arrival in Congress Jeanette was one of a minority of senators who voted against a resolution on declaring war on Germany. Elements within the suffrage movement distanced themselves from her stance and she ultimately failed to win the Republican nomination for her seat at the next election. She chose to stand as an independent candidate but lost.

Jeannette returned to social work, lobbying on social welfare legislation and prevention of war. She re-entered politics as the Second World War loomed and in 1940 was once again elected to the House, where there were now six other women. History seemed to repeat itself when she found herself the only senator to vote against the declaration of war on Japan after the raid on the US naval base at Pearl Harbor in Hawaii. This would be another career-ending vote, with a huge swell of public opinion against her, but Jeannette was defiant, declaring, 'I voted my convictions and redeemed my campaign pledges.'

She never gave up her anti-war stance and in 1968 she led a 5,000-person protest march on Washington against the Vietnam War. She died in 1973 shortly before her ninety-third birthday.

Conkling, Winifred, 'Jeannette Rankin: one woman, one vote', National Park Service, www.nps.gov/articles/000/jeannette-rankin-one-woman-one-vote.htm

'Jeannette Rankin', Britannica, www.britannica.com/biography/
Jeannette-Rankin

'Jeannette Rankin: the first woman member of U.S. Congress', PBS,
8 December 2020, www.pbs.org/wnet/americanmasters/jeannette-
rankin-first-woman-member-us-congress-6r7oqu/15360

'Jeannette Rankin: Nothing left but my integrity', Bill of Rights Institute,
billofrightsinstitute.org/activities/jeanette-rankin-nothing-left-but-
my-integrity-handout-a-narrative

Jones, Martha S., 'For Black women, the 19th Amendment didn't end
their fight to vote', National Geographic, 7 August 2020, www.national
geographic.com/history/article/black-women-continued-fighting-
for-vote-after-19th-amendment

Kratz, Jessie, 'Jeannette Rankin: The woman who voted to give women
the right to vote', U.S. National Archives, 26 January 2017, prologue.
blogs.archives.gov/2017/01/26/jeannette-rankin-the-woman-who-
voted-to-give-women-the-right-to-vote

'Rankin, Jeannette', History, Art & Archives, history.house.gov/People/
Listing/R/RANKIN,-Jeannette-(R000055)

Tucker, Neely, 'Jeannette Rankin and "Shall Not Be Denied: Women Fight
for the Vote"', Library of Congress, 4 June 2019, blogs.loc.gov/loc/
2019/06/draft-new-book-and-exhibition-shall-not-be-denied-women-
fight-for-the-vote

Wilson, Joan Hoff, 'American foreign policy: of her pacifism', Montana the
Magazine of Western History, 1980, montanawomenshistory.org/wp-
content/uploads/2013/11/Wilson-Joan-Peace-is-a-Womans-Job-
Jeannette-Rankin-and-American-Foreign-Policy-the-Origins-of-Her-
Pacifism-r.pdf

Gro Harlem Brundtland

NORWAY

*In 1981 Gro Harlem Brundtland was the first
woman to serve as prime minister of Norway*

Gro Harlem said in her family boys and girls were treated equally
'which was not the regular thing', and she grew up taking it for
granted that equality, social justice and public service was her path
in life. She was born in 1939, in Oslo, to parents who were deeply
embedded in the Labour movement. Her father was a doctor but
would go on to become a government minister, while her mother
worked in the parliamentary group's secretariat. Gro was involved
in party activities from the age of seven.

In 1963 she went to the University of Oslo to study medicine
and met and married her husband while training. Both went on
to study at Harvard University, where Gro received a master's
in public health and then returned to Oslo to work as a public
health officer. She had stepped away from organised politics by
this time, focusing her efforts on the issue of abortion, which
was under intense public debate. It was her strong stance on
abortion rights that brought her to public attention as a leading
advocate for the right of women to choose. Prime Minister Trygve
Bratteli asked to see her after reading her articles in the press.
She said she was shocked to be asked to join the government and
that it hadn't been in her plans. The prime minister invited her
to become the environment minister, not the health minister
as might have seemed logical. She says she realised quickly that
environment policy is also public health policy, and would go on

to make environmental development a cornerstone of her career. Gro became the first woman deputy leader of the Labour Party in 1975 and was elected to the Storting (parliament) in 1977. In 1981, when the Labour prime minister resigned due to illness, Gro was chosen by the party's central committee to take over, making her the youngest person and first woman to become prime minister of Norway. She initially served for only nine months as the party lost the elections held later that year. It was in 1986 that she again became prime minister. She served for three years and was re-elected again in 1990 until she resigned in 1996. It was in her second term that Gro installed what was called the world's first 'women's government' because eight of the eighteen ministers were women. The principle of 40 per cent representation for women, which already existed in some parties, would eventually become the voluntary principle for all the main Norwegian political parties.

In between her terms as prime minister, Gro became chair of the United Nations World Commission on Environment and Development, publishing 'Our Common Future'. Her report introduced the idea of 'sustainable development', a principle that economic growth and social development should meet current needs but not compromise the ability of future generations to meet their own needs. For those future children she set out a challenge for the world to 'listen to the voice of unborn generations and make the earth the hospitable place that any human being deserves'. In 1998 she became director general of the World Health Organization, holding the position during the global pandemics of AIDS and SARS. Gro is a founding member of The Elders, a group of world leaders originally convened by Nelson Mandela to bring their independent expertise to work together for peace, justice and human rights.

Brynildsen, Ida, 'GEC #9 Gro Harlem Brundtland', Future Manager, www.futuremanageralliance.com/gec-9-gro-harlem-brundtland
'Gro Harlem Brundtland', Britannica, www.britannica.com/biography/ Gro-Harlem-Brundtland

'Gro Harlem Brundtland, godmother of sustainable development, born (1939)', Today in Conversation, todayinconservation.com/2018/04/april-20-gro-harlem-brundtland-godmother-of-sustainable-development-born-1939

Skoll.org, 'Gro Harlem Brundtland: I'm a lucky person', YouTube, 23 January 2014, www.youtube.com/watch?v=3_6cL71L870

Maria de Lourdes Pintasilgo

PORTUGAL

In 1979 Maria de Lourdes Pintasilgo was the first
woman to serve as prime minister of Portugal

Maria de Lourdes Pintasilgo grew up knowing no other president than António de Oliveira Salazar, who ruled Portugal as a dictatorship for thirty-six years. She was born in 1930 and her father abandoned the family not long after her birth. Her mother moved them to Lisbon, where Maria showed huge promise in her studies. It was compulsory for young people to attend Salazar's youth organisation, and Maria distinguished herself in the girls' wing, winning the National Prize twice.

At university she chose an engineering degree in industrial chemistry and was one of only three women enrolled on the course. She was politically progressive, though would never commit to one party, and also had a strong religious faith. In her first year of studies, she joined the Female Catholic University Youth and went on to be chair of the group, followed by a stint as president of the Catholic students' organisation.

After graduating she became the first woman engineer at a large Portuguese conglomerate that produced cement. She rose to become chief engineer and then project director. Her decision to leave in 1960 was motivated by her wish to devote herself to social change. She had joined the Grail movement in 1957, a Christian international organisation who saw the women's movement as a way towards peace and justice. She co-founded the Portuguese wing of the group despite strong opposition from the ultra-conservative Catholic Church. Nonetheless, Maria's high profile as a social reformer helped her to become the first woman member of Salazar's Câmera Corporativa, which advised the dictatorship on development and social issues and met in what had been the Senate chamber.

In 1968 Salazar hit his head and fell into a coma. The following years were turbulent as factions grappled for political power, but Maria continued to work in government for women's and social affairs and was a delegate to the United Nations. In 1974 the 'Carnation Revolution' saw left-leaning military officers overthrow the teetering authoritarian regime, paving the way for the transition to democracy.

Maria was appointed secretary of state for social welfare in the provisional government and in 1976 the first democratic elections were held in fifty years. President General António Ramalho Eanes was elected and was accepted by all major parties. In 1979 he asked Maria to be prime minister in the caretaker government until new elections. She continued to refuse membership of any party in order to maintain her independence, but this was of little consequence to conservative MPs, who were furious at her appointment. She told a friend, 'You know, they never forgive me for having dared to enter their world.'

In her short five months in power in an all-male cabinet, she attempted to modernise the limited social welfare system, making social security universal, investing in healthcare, education and labour reforms. A centre-right alliance won the 1980 elections and she stepped down. In 1986 she ran unsuccessfully as an independent candidate for the presidency but with Socialist Party help sat as an independent in the European Parliament from 1987 to 1989.

Maria maintained international respect, advising political leaders and writing numerous books on feminism, religion and economics. In 2001 she established the Fundação Cuidar o Futuro (Take Care of the Future Foundation), which supports programmes that improve people's quality of life. She led the foundation until her death in 2004.

'Maria de Lourdes Pintasilgo', EIGE, eige.europa.eu/lt/women-and-men-inspiring-europe-resource-pool/maria-de-lourdes-pintasilgo

'Maria de Lourdes Pintasilgo', Independent, 14 July 2004, www.independent.co.uk/news/obituaries/maria-de-lourdes-pintasilgo-550094.html

'Maria de Lourdes Pintasilgo', She Thought It, shethoughtit.ilcml.com/biography/maria-de-lourdes-pintasilgo

'Maria de Lourdes Pintasilgo', The Times, 14 July 2004, www.thetimes.co.uk/article/maria-de-lourdes-pintasilgo-ll60pzm2f9n

Skard, Torild, Women of Power: Half a Century of Female Presidents and Prime Ministers Worldwide, Bristol: Policy Press, 2014

Laura Chinchilla

COSTA RICA

In 2010 Laura Chinchilla was the first
woman to be elected president of Costa Rica

Of the more recently elected women in the world, Laura Chinchilla seems to represent a certain figure of the modern democratic state – someone who knew politics and public service would be her career and planned her education around it. She was born in the Costa Rican capital, San José, in 1959 and her father was a senior government official and served as the comptroller general during the 1970s and 1980s.

She earned a degree in public policy from the University of Costa Rica and went on to do a master's in Washington DC in the United States, specialising in institutional reform of the state, the judiciary and the police. She said, 'What most influenced my decision to dedicate myself to public service in my country was that when I turned twenty, while in college, I decided to travel to our neighbouring countries... to witness first-hand the civil wars that were bleeding the region at that time. What I saw hurt me deeply and marked me forever. The brutality, the violence and sadness I witnessed could never be forgotten. Hence, I decided that I would do everything I could to prevent our country from losing the peace and democracy we enjoyed.' She worked as a consultant for non-governmental organisations in the 1980s and 1990s, becoming an expert, writing and lecturing on public safety and human rights.

Her first public role was as minister of public security for centre-left President José María Figueres Olsen of the National Liberation

Party; she was the first woman to hold that position. Between 2002 and 2006 she was elected to the National Congress, where she chaired the Committees on Legal Affairs and Narcotics. Her star continued to rise when in 2006 she was elected vice president. She then resigned in 2008 to concentrate on what she could see as a clear path to the presidency: she was considered a protégée of outgoing President Óscar Arias Sánchez. Rivals accused her of being a puppet of the president and women's groups criticised her for opposing gay marriage and abortion in most cases. But her brand of centrist social conservatism was popular with the public and she won the election with 46.8 per cent of the vote and appointed 39 per cent women to her cabinet.

On her first day she banned opencast mining, created an anti-drug commission and created a national elderly care and infant development network. She faced difficult challenges including a border dispute with Nicaragua, tax reform and accusations of corruption. However, she was proud of her record in reducing crime, particularly homicides, domestic violence and femicide. She earned international awards for her environmental work, and Costa Rica has gone on to be celebrated as a leader in environmental policy.

She ruled out another term in 2014 and went back to working with international organisations. Reflecting on her presidency, she said, 'I believe my major accomplishment was to break the glass ceilings in politics... I visited several schools and found many girls who told me that they too would become, one day, presidents of the country. My election as president certainly contributed to empowering a whole new generation of girls and young women.'

Arias, L., 'Costa Rican President Laura Chinchilla votes in
    Desamparados', *Tico Times*, 2 February 2014, ticotimes.net/2014/02/
    02/costa-ricas-president-laura-chinchilla-votes-in-desamparados
'Ex-president, former finance minister vie for Costa Rica presidency',
    France 24, 7 February 2022, www.france24.com/en/live-news/
    20220207-ex-president-former-finance-minister-vie-for-costa-rica-
    presidency

Hernandez, Daniel, 'Costa Rica welcomes Laura Chinchilla, its first female president', *Los Angeles Times*, 10 May 2010, latimesblogs. latimes.com/laplaza/2010/05/costa-rica.html

'An interview with Laura Chinchilla Miranda, former President of Costa Rica', Leaders, www.leadersmag.com/issues/2021.2_Apr/ Latin-America-Caribbean/LEADERS-Laura-Chinchilla-Miranda-Costa-Rica.html

'Laura Chinchilla', Britannica, www.britannica.com/biography/ Laura-Chinchilla

Skard, Torild, *Women of Power: Half a Century of Female Presidents and Prime Ministers Worldwide*, Bristol: Policy Press, 2014

Iriaka Rātana

NEW ZEALAND

In 1949 Iriaka Rātana was the first Māori woman
to be elected to the New Zealand parliament

Iriaka Te Rio was born in 1905 on the Whanganui River, a sacred place to the Māori people. When she was in her teens, Iriaka's family moved to the Rātana community, the home of the Christian and political Rātana movement. Its leader was Tahupōtiki Wiremu Rātana, a visionary who was challenging the New Zealand prime minister and the British crown. The community was made up of members of Māori tribes who felt dispossessed and came to support the organisation, which sought redress for land confiscations and breaches of a treaty that guaranteed Māori rights.

Iriaka was a talented musician and performer and played in the band that accompanied Rātana on his tours around the country. In 1925 she married him, becoming his second wife, and had two children, losing one to tuberculosis. After the death of her husband in 1939, she married Matiu Rātana, his son by his first marriage. By then, she was one of the most influential women in the Rātana movement, which had become ever more political, allying itself with the country's Labour Party.

With her second husband, she farmed a dairy unit under a Māori land development scheme, and they had six children. When her husband was chosen by the Labour Party to stand as MP for Western Maori in 1945, Iriaka took charge of the farm, milking sixty or more cows and caring for her family of young children.

In 1949 Matiu suffered a serious car accident and died, still only in his thirties. Despite her grief, her farming responsibilities and being heavily pregnant, Iriaka announced her intention to stand in her husband's seat. Her decision met with opposition from some Māori who felt it was wrong for a woman to take the role representing the Western Maori electorate. Te Puea Hērangi, a leader of the Tainui people, criticised Iriaka at a large public meeting, condemning the idea that any woman should 'captain the Tainui canoe'. But Iriaka was selected as the Labour candidate and won the election with a comfortable majority. She gave birth in the weeks after and then entered parliament. She said, 'As the first woman to represent Māori in Parliament, I aim to represent Māori around the country and their varying needs... I aim to end hopelessness for Māori trapped in a descending spiral of poverty, unemployment and lack of education. I believe that these issues can be solved by a caring department of Māori affairs with Māori welfare officers, and other more specialised organisations such as the Māori Women's Welfare League.'

Once in parliament, she focused on social issues, such as housing for the elderly and recently urbanised Māori youth, education and training for Māori, and redevelopment of the Rātana community. In the 1957 election Iriaka had the highest majority in the country and became an advisor to Prime Minister Walter Nash. Iriaka served in the House of Representatives for twenty years. She had a reputation for being polite and positive, and was respected by both sides of the House. It wasn't until 1967 that another Māori woman joined her in parliament.

She retired from parliament in 1969, returning to her farm, wearing her gumboots, going to the races and weaving korowai (Māori cloaks). She died in 1981, survived by nine children and many grandchildren.

'Iriaka Rātana', New Zealand History, nzhistory.govt.nz/people/
    iriaka-ratana
'Iriaka Matiu Rātana', Wahine Honoa, wahinehonoa.weebly.com/
    iriaka-matiu-ratana.html

'Iriaka Rātana (1905–1981)', toti, www.toti.co.nz/he-tangata-project/
dame-hilda-ross/iriaka-ratana

'Iriaka Rātana – first wahine Māori MP', New Zealand Parliament,
29 November 2019, www.parliament.nz/en/get-involved/features/
iriaka-ratana-first-wahine-maori-mp

'Story: Rātana Church – Te Haahi Rātana', TEARA, teara.govt.nz/en/
ratana-church-te-haahi-ratana

'Story: Rātana, Iriaka Matiu', TEARA, teara.govt.nz/en/biographies/5r7/
ratana-iriaka-matiu

Marie Juchacz

GERMANY

*In 1919 Marie Juchacz was one of the first thirty-seven
women elected to the Weimar National Assembly, and she
was the first woman to address a German parliament*

When Marie Juchacz stepped up to speak at the Weimar National
Assembly, she pulled no punches, declaring, 'We German women
are not bound to thank this government in the traditional sense.
What this government has done is only natural. It has given women
what they had hitherto wrongfully been denied.' Women had only
got the vote three months earlier, something Marie had campaigned for tirelessly.

Marie was born into relative poverty in 1879. She was able to go
to the local school but had to leave at fourteen to support her family
after her father fell ill with a lung infection. She worked as a maid
and then day and night in a factory that made fishing nets; she later
wrote, 'I still remember with horror, the misery of this night work.'
It was these early experiences combined with the influence of her
brother, who introduced her to political books, that fostered her
lifelong interest in social change.

She found an apprenticeship as a dressmaker, taking a job with
the tailor Bernhard Juchacz, whom she married in 1903. They had
two children, but the marriage was unhappy and they divorced at a
time when this came with significant stigma. She moved to Berlin
with her children and her younger sister, Elisabeth Kirschmann-
Röhl, and her children. She was a divorced single parent and their
household was an unconventional one for the time.

When a law was repealed allowing women to join political parties, Marie joined the Social Democratic Party and was quickly recognised as a popular speaker. She won a paid role in the party in 1913 and rose to be women's secretary on the executive committee. When women won the right to vote and stand for election, Marie and her sister were two of the first women to win seats in the Weimar National Assembly in 1919. In the Reichstag (parliament) Marie pushed for the protection of mothers, for change in the legal status of illegitimate children, and for reform of the Divorce Act, which gave women no right to decide on the number or planning of the children they had.

In addition to this, on behalf of the party Marie founded the workers' welfare organisation Arbeiterwohlfahrt (AWO). The AWO's role was to support those displaced and destitute due to the First World War, particularly working-class families, often in the form of self-help, by and for working-class women. As its chair, Marie built a remarkable organisation with training facilities for social workers, kindergartens and convalescent homes. The AWO had around 1,414 advice centres when the Nazi Party shut it down in 1933.

The Nazis dissolved all political parties and persecuted their leaders and members. Marie and her sister fled, eventually migrating to the United States. There she founded Arbeiterwohlfahrt USA – Help for the Victims of National Socialism, which provided support in the form of care parcels for devastated Germany after the end of the Second World War. In 1949 Marie returned to Germany to continue her social welfare work. When she died in 1956, the AWO said, 'Her entire life was in the service of the struggle for a better and more just world.'

Breuer, Rayna, 'Marie Juchacz: A life for justice and equality', DW, 19 February 2019, www.dw.com/en/marie-juchacz-a-life-for-justice-and-equality/a-47038486

'Juchacz, Marie (1879–1956)', Encyclopedia.com, www.encyclopedia. com/women/encyclopedias-almanacs-transcripts-and-maps/ juchacz-marie-1879-1956

'Marie Juchacz', Gedenkstätte Deutscher Widerstand, www.gdw-berlin.
de/en/recess/biographies/index_of_persons/biographie/view-bio/
marie-juchacz/?no_cache=1

'Marie Juchacz (1879–1956)', Towards Emancipation?, hist259.web.unc.
edu/marie-juchacz-1879-1956

'Marie Juchacz, geb. Gohlke (1879–1956)', Frankfurter Fraunzimmer,
www.frankfurterfrauenzimmer.de/ep10-detail.html?bio=dt

'Marie Juchacz – the first woman to speak in parliament', The Federal
Government, www.bundesregierung.de/breg-en/chancellor/marie-
juchacz-the-first-woman-to-speak-in-parliament-1582438

Quataert, Jean H., Reluctant Feminists in German Social Democracy, 1885–1917,
Princeton: Princeton University Press, 2015, p. 44

Striewski, Jennifer, 'Marie Juchacz', Portal Rheinische Geschichte,
www.rheinische-geschichte.lvr.de/Persoenlichkeiten/marie-juchacz/
DE-2086/lido/57c92fddc69b11.62149235

Jahanara Shahnawaz

INDIA

In 1937 Jahanara Shahnawaz was the first woman to serve as a parliamentary secretary in the Punjab Legislative Assembly

Jahanara Shahnawaz showed early promise as a social reformer. At age nine she wrote her first article, 'A Female Education', which was published in an Islamic weekly magazine for women. She had been born in Lahore in northern India in 1896 to an affluent Punjabi family. She attended school, encouraged by her parents, and her upbringing was influenced by her mother's rejection of the restrictions of purdah, like a number of urban, middle-class women. Purdah is a religious and social practice of female seclusion either by physical segregation in the home or through clothing. Her father was one of the founders of the All-India Muslim League and an elder statesman of the British government of India.

When she was fifteen Jahanara's parents married her to Mian Muhammad Shahnawaz, the widower of an aunt. Despite her marriage, Jahanara went on to higher education at Queen Mary College in Lahore and, with the help of the principal, completed her studies following the birth of her first daughter in 1912. Four years later she published the novel *Hasanara Begum* about the struggles of a girl whose house and property are taken by her relatives when her parents die because women had no right to inherit.

In 1918 Jahanara successfully moved the All-India Muslim Women's Conference to pass a resolution against polygamy and in 1927 she was at the forefront of successful lobbying to raise the minimum legal age for marriage, setting it at fourteen for girls and eighteen for boys. She came to London in 1930 for a round table conference on India's constitutional development. She lobbied hard for Indian women's right to vote and for women to have reserved seats in the legislature. When the Government of India Act 1935 was finally published it gave voting rights to almost 600,000 women, with eighty women going on to be elected to provincial assemblies in 1937. Jahanara herself was elected to the Punjab Legislative Assembly and became parliamentary secretary of education and public health.

The Indian independence movement had been active throughout Jahanara's life and was coming to a head. She was part of the movement that wanted independence but also the creation of Pakistan to protect the political interests of Indian Muslims. The elections of 1946 were seen as a test of the Muslim League's mandate for Pakistan, and their majority in the legislature greatly accelerated her party's demands. Despite this, the governor of Punjab asked the Unionist leader to form the provincial ministry, which led to the civil disobedience movement in Punjab, and Jahanara was arrested along with other Muslim League leaders. Ongoing agitation was part of the picture that paved the way for the partition plan and the establishment of Pakistan in August 1947.

After partition, refugee women and children arriving in Pakistan suffered enormously and Jahanara worked to address their needs. In 1948 she led a protest of thousands of women in the streets of Lahore, demanding better economic rights for women. The Muslim Personal Law of Shariat was passed, finally recognising women's right to inherit property, the very issue the character in Jahanara's novel had suffered from over thirty years before and possibly her greatest achievement for women. Jahanara Shahnawaz died in 1979 at age eighty-three.

Ahmad, Dr Riaz, 'Muslim Punjab's Fight for Pakistan', *Pakistan Journal of History & Culture*, 28 (1), 2007, www.nihcr.edu.pk/Downloads/Punjab_Muslim.pdf

Ali, Azra Asghar and Tariq, Shahnaz, 'Begum Jahanara Shahnawaz and the socio-cultural uplift of Muslim women in British India', JRSP, 45 (2), 2008, pu.edu.pk/images/journal/history/Current%20Issues/ Azra%20Asghar%20Ali%20&%20Shahnaz%20Tariq.pdf

'Begum Shah Nawaz', Story of Pakistan, storyofpakistan.com/begum-shah-nawaz

British Movietone, 'Begum Shah Nawaz Talks to You', YouTube, 21 July 2015, www.youtube.com/watch?v=jRdppb6zPxw

'Conferencing the International', University of Nottingham, www. nottingham.ac.uk/research/groups/conferencing-the-international/ delegates/people.aspx?id=6e6b1852-c5be-40ca-97b7-9ab00136af65

Ghosh, Partha S., 'Women in politics', Times of India, 14 December 2006, timesofindia.indiatimes.com/edit-page/women-in-politics/article show/807009.cms

Hussain, Sabiha, 'Muslim women's rights discourse in the pre-independence period', www.cwds.ac.in/wp-content/uploads/2016/09/ MuslimWomensRights.pdf

Lahora Museum photo collection, 'Leading from the front (March, 1947)', Friday Times, 1 June 2018, www.thefridaytimes.com/leading-from-the-front-march-1947

Minault, Gail, 'Coming out: decisions to leave Purdah', Second Nature: Women and the Family, 23 (3/4), winter 1996, pp. 93–105, www.jstor. org/stable/23004613

Salim, Saquib, 'Begum Jahanara Shahnawaz: who won the political rights for the Indian women', Heritage Times, 12 September 2020, heritagetimes.in/begum-jahanara-shahnawaz-who-won-the-political-rights-for-the-indian-women

Singh, Nagendra Kr (ed.), Encyclopaedia of Women Biography: India, Pakistan, Bangladesh, India: A.P.H. Publishing Corporation, 2001, p. 89

Eugenia Charles

DOMINICA

*In 1980 Eugenia Charles was the first woman
to be elected prime minister of Dominica*

Mary Eugenia Charles was born in 1919 in Pointe Michel, Dominica, which was under British colonial rule. Eugenia's grandparents had been enslaved and though her parents came from humble farming backgrounds, her father's success as a fruit exporter, and later as a banker, placed her family in what was known as the 'coloured bourgeoisie' in a society which still strongly revered class and colour. She had access to the Caribbean island's only secondary education for girls, a convent-run school. She says many people thought her father was the 'strong man' but actually her mother was 'the boss of the family' and wasn't satisfied unless Eugenia came first in her class.

While learning shorthand by attending the local magistrates' court, she became interested in law, and then worked as an assistant to a magistrate in the Colonial Legal Service. In 1947 she moved to Toronto to attend university, following that with a law degree from the London School of Economics, after which she became a barrister. In 1949 she returned to Dominica to support her ageing parents, setting up a successful legal chambers in Roseau and becoming the first Dominican woman to practise law and be called to the island's Bar.

Eugenia was nearly fifty when she began her career in politics. The island was self-governing by this time but had yet to achieve independence. In the late 1960s the Dominican government introduced legislation limiting dissent, and Eugenia was among those alarmed by the curb on rights, including freedom of the press and the right to criticise the government. Those opposed to the changes labelled it the 'Shut Your Mouth Bill' and in 1968 Eugenia was part of the group who formed the new Dominica Freedom Party (DFP), a broad-based party made up of opposition politicians.

Eugenia entered the House of Assembly as a nominated member in 1970, and won a seat in the 1975 general election and became leader of the opposition. Eugenia hadn't married or had children and frequently faced personal attacks from government politicians, such as accusations that she lacked understanding of women's realities because she had never felt the pain of childbirth. After pointing out that none of the male MPs had felt it either, she says she learned to ignore the abuse completely and argued that it actually garnered her support from women and voters who disliked this style of politics. Gaining in popularity, in 1980 the DFP won the elections and Eugenia became prime minister. She also served as her own foreign affairs minister and finance and development minister.

She is credited with stabilising Dominica's political turmoil, fighting government corruption and bringing electricity, roads and water to the whole island. She survived several coup attempts, including by former prime minister Patrick John. She said, 'If people can't get you by the ballot box, they will try to get you by the bullet.' She consequently developed a fearless reputation and weathered the storms of these attacks, going on to win two additional terms as prime minister, in 1985 and 1990. Eventually her brand of prudent conservatism fell out of favour and she retired when her party lost in 1995. She returned to her law practice and became involved in former US president Jimmy Carter's election monitoring organisation, the Carter Centre, before her death in 2005.

Commonwealth Secretariat, *Women in Politics: Voices from the Commonwealth*, UK: Commonwealth Secretariat, 1999

'Eugenia Charles', Britannica, www.britannica.com/biography/ Eugenia-Charles

'Eugenia Charles', University of London, london.ac.uk/eugenia-charles

'From the archives (video): Dame Eugenia Charles, being interviewed in 1996', Dominica News Online, 28 June 2020, dominicanewsonline. com/news/homepage/news/from-the-archives-video-dame-eugenia-charles-being-interviewed-in-1996

'History revisited: BBC television interview of Mary Eugenia Charles', TheDominican.net, 14 May 2015, www.thedominican.net/2015/05/bbc-interviews-eugenia-charles.html

'Hon Dame Eugenia Charles (LLM, 1949)', LSE, www.lse.ac.uk/law/centenary/people/eugenia-charles

Pattullo, Polly, 'Dame Eugenia Charles', Guardian, 8 September 2005, www.theguardian.com/news/2005/sep/08/guardianobituaries.pollypattullo

Dilma Rousseff

BRAZIL

In 2011 Dilma Rousseff was the first woman to serve as president of Brazil

Dilma Rousseff's fall from power is still so recent that it's difficult to assess what her long-term legacy will be. Some say she was the first politician in Brazil that it wasn't possible to corrupt, others say that's of no benefit if she knew corruption was happening. Born in 1947 in Belo Horizonte to a prosperous family, she became a socialist at secondary school and then a student leader.

After a coup in 1964 by the armed forces, she took part in leftist guerrilla movements against the military dictatorship. She met and married lawyer Carlos Araujo and they were both arrested for their activities. Dilma was imprisoned for three years and was subjected to beatings, electric shocks and other forms of torture. Together with her husband she went on to found the Democratic Labour Party, and as the grip of the dictatorship weakened, she became active in local politics. She divorced in 2001 and switched to the Workers' Party, supporting Luiz Inácio Lula da Silva (commonly known as Lula) as president. In 2002 President Lula appointed her minister of energy, and after he was no longer able to run he supported Dilma as his successor.

In the 2010 presidential election Dilma campaigned on the promise of economic stability, reducing inequality and eradicating extreme poverty. She won with 56 per cent of the vote and when she took office she signed a landmark law that established a truth commission to investigate the disappearances and human rights abuses during military rule.

Accusations of corruption were present from the first year of her tenure. Five cabinet ministers, all veterans from the Lula administration, resigned. At the same time a political corruption trial on bribes to members of the Chamber of Deputies was running, and Lula was allegedly involved. In tandem, the Brazilian economy was slowing and the football World Cup was due to be delivered in 2014, followed by the 2016 Olympic Games in Rio, placing significant strains on public finances. Huge demonstrations spread across the country and Dilma's popularity dropped.

She faced a massive challenge to secure a second term in office but achieved it with 51 per cent of the vote in the second round; however, the scandals were not over. It was suggested billions were passed off in kickbacks from state oil giant Petrobras to private construction firms, business leaders and politicians when Dilma was chair of Petrobras while energy minister. An investigation cleared her of wrongdoing and even her opponents acknowledged her status as an honest politician, but many Brazilians doubted that she could have been unaware of the corruption. In addition to the Petrobras scandal, accusations arose that Dilma had presided over misuse of state bank funds to mask budget deficits.

Huge anti-government demonstrations took place, this time demanding Dilma's impeachment. In the Brazilian Senate, Dilma gave a powerful defence of herself while being questioned for fourteen hours. Ultimately the Senate voted to remove her. Far-right politician Jair Bolsonaro dedicated his pro-impeachment vote specifically to the army colonel who had tortured her.

On the reasons for her downfall she said, 'The fact that I was the first woman president was a factor in what happened to me... It wasn't 100 per cent because of that. But it was a component.' With optimism she said, 'I think it will be easier for the next woman president.'

'Brazil's President Dilma Rousseff makes her mark', BBC, 29 December 2011, www.bbc.co.uk/news/world-latin-america-16288184

'Dilma Rousseff', Britannica, www.britannica.com/biography/
Dilma-Rousseff

'Dilma Rousseff', Brown University Library, library.brown.edu/create/
fivecenturiesofchange/chapters/chapter-8/dilma-rousseff

'Dilma Rousseff impeachment: How did it go wrong for her?', BBC,
12 May 2016, www.bbc.co.uk/news/world-latin-america-36028247

Skard, Torild, *Women of Power: Half a Century of Female Presidents and Prime
Ministers Worldwide*, Bristol: Policy Press, 2014

Acknowledgements

I'd like to offer my sincerest thanks to Joelle Owusu, who commissioned me to write *Women Who Won*, understanding that this book was at the intersection of all my skills and interests – I'm incredibly grateful you found me. Huge thanks to DeAndra Lupu for your support and for calmly shepherding me through the editorial process with the kind of clear communication that someone with a short attention span really appreciates. Further thanks to the team at Unbound past and present, including Katy Guest, Cassie Waters and Georgia Odd for making this book a reality.

Huge credit for the final product must go to Emmy Lupin, who is such a vibrant illustrator, bringing my profiles of historical women to life in a modern and accessible way. Thank you, Emmy. Thanks also to Mark Ecob for your strong design which makes me feel positive about politics – a not inconsiderable feat sometimes. Thank you, Patty Rennie, for your text design.

Thanks to Simon Auckland for your generous sponsorship, though you take no credit in the front of the book; your spontaneity in choosing to help is to the benefit of others, thank you. Thanks in the same vein to Stefan Cross, a man who works for equality and took a chance on a stranger's tweet. Thank you, Laura Yates at Clifford Chance, for being a great ally. Thanks to the Jo Cox Foundation for the important work they do; I am proud to be associated with an organisation that works for civility in politics when we need it more than ever. I hope Jo would have liked this book.

I am forever grateful for my friends, family, colleagues and strangers on the internet who stepped up to support this book. Fundraising was wildly outside of my comfort zone and every time someone pledged to support the book, I felt able to keep going.

Biggest thanks to my partner, James, who supports me in all my many side-projects by being an equal partner in our home and our lives. Thank you, Jamma. Thank you, Josie and Clem, for being so fabulous and the reason that I am ambitious for myself – I hope it paves the way for you to be ambitious for yourselves.

A Note on the Author

ROS BALL was born in Bedfordshire and studied at Goldsmiths College in London. She spent many years as a journalist at the BBC in Westminster, where her short historical films were a regular feature on BBC Parliament. In 2017 she published her first book, *The Gender Agenda*, a two-year diary of the way the world treats her daughter and son differently. Ros lives in London with her family and works for the civil service.

@Rosball

A Note on the Illustrator

EMMY LUPIN is a Nottingham-based illustrator working under the moniker Emmy Lupin Studio. Specialising in digital illustration that's big on pattern and colour, Emmy's work is inspired by looking at life through a female lens. Emmy has been commissioned by the likes of Adidas, TikTok, *Stylist Magazine*, Adobe, Three UK and SEGA, to name a few. Emmy also has a shop selling prints, cards and other lovely things.

www.emmylupin.com
@emmylupinstudio

Unbound is the world's first crowdfunding publisher, established in 2011.

We believe that wonderful things can happen when you clear a path for people who share a passion. That's why we've built a platform that brings together readers and authors to crowdfund books they believe in – and give fresh ideas that don't fit the traditional mould the chance they deserve.

This book is in your hands because readers made it possible. Everyone who pledged their support is listed below. Join them by visiting unbound.com and supporting a book today.

Syeda Ali
Jen Allerton
Nicola Alloway
Paula Álvarez Vaccaro
Catherine Anderson
Helen Anderson
Anna and Jane
Helen Antrobus
Rebecca Asher
Martyn Atkins
Louisa Attaheri
Anna Auckland
Edie Auckland
Ellis Auckland
Nengi Ayika
James Aylett
Rozhana Azra
Louise Bailey
Lin Ball
Penelope Ball
Peter Ball
Brian Ballantyne
Sakina Ballard
James Barber
Hannah Bardell
Fiona M Barham
Sally Barnes
Peter Barratt
Emily Batchelor
Dianne Bateman
Val Bayliss-Brideaux
Nancy Baynes
Betsy Bearden
Bedford Girls' School
    and The Alumnae

Mashkura Begum
Mathew Belcher
Emily Bell
M Bell
Carolyn Belson
Richard Benjamin
Natalie Bennett
Neil Bennett
Phillip Bennett-
    Richards
Fiona Berry
Miranda Bertram
Leah Bevan-Haines
Anna Birch
Rachel Birrell
David Black
Simon Bleasdale
Stevie Blue
Tessa Boase
Caroline Bolton
Alison Bonny
Kate Boulton
Daisy Bow Du Toit
Suzannah Brecknell
Ailish Breen
Kate Bridgman
Amy Brocklehurst
Martha-Louise Browell
Jago Brown
Kitty Brown
Brian Browne
Teresa Broxton
Eddie Buckley
Liz Burgess
Catrina Burke

Joy Burnford
Faye Burnie
Tiffany Burrows
Mia Burt
Sue Butcher
Rachel Byrne
Cara C.
Vanessa Cairns
Susanne Cameron-
    Nielsen
Laura Carey
Livia Carlini Schmidt
Jessamy Carlson
Lisa Carr
Matt Castanier
Angela Chaggar
Jas Chahal
Debbie Challis
Clifford Chance
Susha Chandrasekhaar
Becky Chantry
Hannah
    Charalambous
Sarah Childs
Alex Chisholm
Jessica Chivers
Rachel Clack
Deborah Clair
Kate Clanchy
Helen Clancy
Tom Clancy
Giovanna Clark
Ali Clay
Jen Clayton
Grant Clemence

Cris Cloyd
Deborah Coltham
Helen Cook
Carly Cooper
Ginny Cooper
Nick Cooper
Poppy Coppins
Dr Helen Corbett
Cecilia Cordeiro
Jodie Cosh
Elizabeth Coulter
Serena Cowdy
Patrick Cowling
Krista Cowman
Gaynor Cox
Amy Craik
Deborah Crawford
Lucy Crawford
Tomas Cronholm
Rachel Crosby
Serena Cross
Crosshall Junior
    School
Cat Crossley
Jessica Crowe
John Crowther
Martine Croxall
Mark Cumisky
Rosalin Cummings
Rachel Cummings-
    Dunn
Alexander Cunliffe
George Dalton
Damesnet
Roger Davidson

SUPPORTERS

Chris Davies
Matt Davies
Jess Day
Jasmin De Freitas
Joanne Deeming
Dana Denis-Smith
Alice Devlin
Anthony Diakou
Olivia Dickinson
Claire Dickson
Lianne Dillsworth
Ian Dinwiddy
Lisa Donoghue
(from Mark and
Christina)
Alys Dow
Sandy Driskell
Clare Dryhurst
Jane Duffus
Roy Duncan
Michael Dunn
Sheila Dunn
Elizabeth Dwiar
Naomi Eden
Jen Edwards
Amy Elizabeth
Imogen Ely
Rachel Erskine
Huw Evana
Amanda Evans
Jane Evans
John Evans
Claire Evenden
Darcey & Holly Feeney
Edwin Flay
Anne Fletton
For All Women
Louise Ford
Sam Francis
Tristan Frayling
Bridget Frost
Jo Froude
Jonathan Gadsby
Josephine Gale
Cristina Galindo
Sarah Gammon
Penny Gane
Mandy Garner
Ella Garrett
Louise Gibbard
Julie Gibbon
Daniele Gibney
Michaela Gibson
Ann Gilpin
Mandy Girling
Steven Gislam
Julie Gittoes
Miriam Glover
Kirsty Gogan
Julie Gottlieb

Julie Gough
Claire Gould
Caroline Gourlay
Kirsty Grainger
Anne Grant
Fiona Grant
Louise Granville Smith
Alex Graul
Samuel Gray
Emma Green
Esther Green
Isabel Green
Jen Green
Tony Grew
Judith Griffith
Cathy Groves
Rachel Guest
Georgia Gunderson
Ley-Anne Haigh-
Forsyth
Jessica Hallett
Emma Halliday
Laura Hamblyn
Chrissy Hamlin
Vanessa Hammick
Bridget Hargreave
Robin Hargreaves
Siobhan Harley
Harris Academy
Peckham
Amanda Harrison
Peter Harrison
Toni Harrison
Vanessa Harrison-Gill
Tom Hart
Emma Hartfield
Gillian Harvey-Bush
Helen Hayes
Alice Heggie
Caia Henderson
Emma-Kate Henry
Lucy Henzell-Thomas
Anna Hepworth
Harriet Herbert
Imogen Herbert
Kate Herbert
Duncan Hess
Lucy Higgins
Emily JS Higgins &
Georgina E Flaxman
James Higgott
Jaine Hilston
Nick Hilton
Emily Hodder
Katie Hogg
Ellen Hohbach Scheetz
Stephen Holbrook
Ailsa Holland
Holly Holmes
Laura Holmes

Helen Hood
Ola Hotson
Lorraine Howard
Helen Hubert
Dr Elin Huckerby –
Congratulations
on your PhD!
Alexandra Hughes-
Johnson
Susan Hulme
Caroline Hunt
Julian Huppert
John Hutton
Vicky Iglikowski-Broad
Shubeeh Imam
Mike Indian
Michelle Jackson
Aiden James
Louise James
Alice Jefferis
Ernest Jenavs
Lyndsey Jenkins
Anna Jessop
Marjorie Johns
Katie Rowley Jones
Roger Jones
Nick Kampa
Dr Nikita Kanani
Kea and Kiwi
Lisa Keane Elliott
William Kedjanyi
Robert Keeling
Samantha Kenny
Fozia Khanam
Dan Kieran
Sarah King
Kerry Kissinger
Tertia-Jayne Klein
Karen Klomp
Peter Knowles
Leyla & Ava Kozton
Helene Kreysa
Debbie Kurup
Paul La Planche
Nicolas Laborie
Dr Mira Lal
Felicity Lane
Nina Lawrence
Emily Lawson
Becky Laxton-Bass
Sarah Layton
Jessica Leach
Swee Leng Harris
Isi Leslie
Anastasia Lewis
Catrin Lewis
Susan Lewis
Michala Liavaag
Felicity Liggins
Stephanie Lilley

Jonathan Littlemore
Jonathan Russell Lloyd
Samantha Lloyd
Ana Lockerbie
Camille Lofters
Stuart Long
Emily Lowden
Isaac Lowe
Rosemary Mac Cabe
Orla Mackle
Sheila MacNeill
Claire Madge
Hajira Mahomed
Di Mainstone
Catt** Makin
Joshua Mallalieu
Anne Mallek
Philippa Manley
Chris Mann
Liz Marin-Curtoud
Lucy Mark
Alice Marks
Anabel Marsh
Elaine Martel
Charlotte Martin
Sarah Matheson
LK Matthews
Sukie Matthews
Caroline Mayes
Charlotte Maynard
Liam McAlinden
Elysia McCaffrey
Steve McCaffrey
Pamela McCarthy
Lawrence McCrossan
Marie McGinley
Garry McQuinn
Ineke Meijer
Nick Mellish
Jill Meyers
James Millar
John Millar
Richard Millar
Susan Millar
Clem Millar-Ball
Josie Millar-Ball
Ciara Minnitt
John Mitchinson
Mira MJ
Megha Mohan
Linda Monckton
Romy Morgan
Amelia Morris
Fionnuala Morris
Kate Mosse
Rachel Muers
Sumita Mukherjee
Gillian Murphy
Olivia & Isabella
Murray

Carlo Navato
Abbie Naylor
Michael Neale
Antony Nelson
Daisy Nelson
Charlotte Nettleton
Chris Newsom and
Jasmine Milton
Catherine Nicholls
Sue Nieland
Stacey Nievweija
Katherine Nightingale
Laura Mae Nuttall
Carolyn O'Connor
Sara O'Connor
Steve O'Gorman
Lisa O'Hare
Fiona O'Neill
Mark O'Neill
Beryl Oakes
Katharine Oakes
Emily Oakes-Whiffin
Traci Oliveira
Joelle Owusu-Sekyere
Helen Pankhurst
Steph Parker
Diana Parkes
Alex Partridge
Tracey Partridge
Anna Patterson
Lucy Pattison
Naomi Paxton
Liam Payne
Naomi Pearson-Tagg
Anni Peckham
Liv Pennington
Amy Perry
Tim Perry
Rebecca Peyton
Chrysi Philalithes
Jennifer Pierce
Mark Pinnes
Sarah Pinnes
Anne Plouffe
Justin Pollard
Nicole Ponsford
Alison Potter
Kate Powling
Miriam Price
Naomi Purkiss
Elliott Rae
Susie Ramroop
Edward Randall
Veronika Rasickaite
Alex Reed
Hazel Reeves
Leisa Reichelt
Alex Rejstrand

Anne Reyersbach
Neil Ridulfa
Jessica Riley
Liam Riley
Euan Ritchie
Pamela Ritchie
Cristina Rivadulla-
Rey
Alysha Roake
Mary Robb
Bethan Roberts
David Roberts
Jenny Roberts
Kate Roberts
Caroline Roberts-
Cherry
Craig Robertson
Jo-ann Robertson
Jane Robinson
Val Rogers
Charlotte Rose
Lin Rose
Georgina Rosen
Rosie Ross
Jane Rossin and Jen
Edwards
Miranda Roszkowski
Ruby Rousson
Alexandra Runswick
Lucy Russell
Pookie Russell
Sophia Russell
Sabrina Russo
Casey Ryan
Cris Saunders
Andy Sawford
Tim Saxton
Angela Scarlett-
Newcomen
Anja Schmidt
Ramona Schneider
Heather Scott
Kim Seath
Ann-Marie Sefton
Joseph Seliga
Daniel Sewell
Keela Shackell-Smith
MBE
Leah Shearer
Liz Sheppard
Lucy Sheppard
Lisbet Sherlock
Gavin Sherriff
Hilary Silk
Sophy Silver
Andrew Simcock
Juliet Simmons
Veronica Skidmore

Catherine Skowron
Duncan Smith
Kathryn Smith
Emma Smy
Hetty Sparkles
Hilary Spencer
Penny Spiller
Tatton Spiller
Laura Spink
Wendy Staden
Kate Stafford
Louise Stafford
Isabel Stainsby
Keris Stainton
CJ Stanley
Lara Stanley
Jenny Staples
Charlotte Stemp
Ruth Stevens
Jacqui A Stewart
Lyndsay Stewart
Allison Strachan
Corrine Streetly
Sheila Sturgeon
Pauline Subran
Lizzie Summerskill
Dan Sumption
Francesca Sutton
Louise Sutton
Jo Swinson
Maariyah Syeda
Gila Tabrizi
Mari Takayanagi
Christine Talmage
Nicola Tanner
Alison Tansey
Lisa Taylor
Rosalind Taylor-Hook
Max Tchanturia
Renée Teate
Ursula Tebbet-Duffin
Katy Theakston
Dolly Theis
Lucy Thomas
Margery Thomas
Kim Thornhill
Kim Thornton
Natalie Threlfall
Cecilia Thwaites
Claire Tillotson
Karin Tischler
Pippa Tolfts
Louise Toner
Dylan Topham
Lee Topley
Sabine Tötemeyer
Moira Townsend
Tessa Trabue

Jennifer Tracey
Melody Travers
Gareth Trufitt
Maisie Turley
Jacqui Turner
Audrey Uhlmann
Sophia Ukor
nicole valentinuzzi
Patricia van den Akker
Armida van Rij
S. van Rossenberg
Zach Van Stanley
Felicity van
Steenbergen
Simon Vaughan
Alejandro Villalobos
Gillian Waddilove
Lindsay Walker
Andrew Walsh
Maria Walton
Campagna
Deb Waters
Joanna Watson
Lizzie Watson
Rebecca Watt
Angela Watts
Andrew Weaver
Lisa Webb
Esther Webber
Lee Webster
Sarah Welfare
Alexandra Welsby
Mathilde Wennevold
Kate Whannel
Anna Wharton
Anna White
Rebeccca White
Gill Whitehead
Carol Ann Whitehead
FRSA
Maggie Whittle
Cat Wildman
Tom Willetts
Lucy Williams
Sarah Williams
Catherine Williamson
Emma Wilson
Tatiana Withanage
Edward Wood
Karen Wood
Claudia Woodlingfield
John Worne
Shereen Yala-Callum
Carolyn Yates
Huw and Luke Young
K Zog

292